Failure by Design

The Story behind America's Broken Economy

Failure by Design

The Story behind America's Broken Economy

Josh Bivens

Foreword by
Lawrence Mishel

ECONOMIC POLICY INSTITUTE

ILR Press
an imprint of Cornell University Press
Ithaca and London

ISBN 978-0-8014-5015-0 (cloth: alk. paper)

Printed in the United States of America

Recommended citation for this book is as follows: Bivens, Josh. *Failure by Design: The Story behind America's Broken Economy*. An Economic Policy Institute Book. Ithaca, N.Y.: ILR Press, an imprint of Cornell University Press, 2011

Cornell University Press strives to use environmentally responsible suppliers and materials to the fullest extent possible in the publishing of its books. Such materials include vegetable-based, low-VOC inks and acid-free papers that are recycled, totally chlorine-free, or partly composed of nonwood fibers. For further information, visit our website at www.cornellpress.cornell.edu.

Cloth printing 10 9 8 7 6 5 4 3 2 1

Jacket design: Kieran Daly of Winking Fish   Front cover illustration: Eric Shansby

 (28)

Table of Contents

List of Figures

A note on data sources and methods for the figures in this book
Most of the figures in this book are drawn from previous editions of *The State of Working America*. Those that are taken from other research are cited as such and a bibliography provided at the end of the book. For those readers interested in learning more about the sources and methods behind the construction of these charts, see the *State of Working America* Web site (www.StateOfWorkingAmerica.org). This book uses "typical" to mean median, that is, the family or worker in the exact middle of the distribution.

Acknowledgments

It surprises me that even with the slimmest of books one accumulates a mountain of debts, but so it goes. Although almost all of the larger insights in this book are channeled directly from conversations with other EPI researchers and writers, both past and present, I hesitate to list them because I might forget some. Among current EPI research staff, Kathryn Edwards, Kai Filion, Elise Gould, Andrew Green, Larry Mishel, and Heidi Shierholz all produced charts, provided data, or reviewed numbers for the book. Ross Eisenbrey, Jody Franklin, John Irons, and Joe Procopio all read the manuscript and offered helpful suggestions as well as generally helped keep the whole endeavor moving down the tracks. Anna Turner served as overall general manager for the book—producing graphs, tracking down data, reviewing the text, and fact checking everything. It probably would've been very little extra work for her to have written the whole thing.

Despite all the valuable assistance I received, any bungles in translation are strictly mine.

Finally, Holley and Finn continue to provide more-than-plausible excuses as to why I've yet to reach my full professional potential, and for this I couldn't be happier.

Foreword

For more than 20 years *The State of Working America* has provided an unvarnished look at the living standards of low- and middle-income Americans. Along the way, it has established a reputation as the gold standard in tracking trends in income, wages, hours, jobs, and inequality, leading the *Financial Times* to call it "the most comprehensive independent analysis of the U.S. labor market." This effort has reflected two core values of the Economic Policy Institute since its founding: (1) a belief that judgments on how well the economy is performing should depend upon whether it is delivering rising living standards to the vast majority; and (2) the importance of empirical documentation as the basis for economic policy.

More often than not over these 20 years, *The State of Working America* has detailed the data behind an economy that was not working particularly well for working Americans. Even during times of respectable economic growth for the nation as whole, typical families' living standards grew sluggishly. There were exceptions, to be sure. The late 1990s saw low unemployment that provided even workers at the bottom-end of the wage scale with the bargaining power they needed to demand raises, and wage growth across the board was rapid and equitable.

Outside this brief window, however, the story of the American economy since *The State of Working America*'s inception has been largely one of unfulfilled promise, with overall growth failing to translate into prosperity for most because the fruits of this growth were concentrated only among those at the very top of the income ladder.

For 11 editions, *The State of Working America* has documented the facts behind these trends, charting the rapid rise of economic inequality and the much-less rapid rise of wages for most Americans. It has largely hewn to pure documentation, with little narrative or policy prescription. However, after more than 20 years of growing economic inequality and the worst recession since World War II, it became increasingly clear to us at the Economic Policy Institute that there was an economic narrative hidden between the lines of all the admittedly dry data. But, like the visual puzzles that embed a big picture in repeating patterns of shapes that obscure it, this story may not be obvious to those not looking for it or those who just weren't looking at the right angle.

Consequently, instead of a single massive tome, this latest incarnation of *The State of Working America* is a bundle of products, both print and electronic. Most of the data that the book's habitual users have become accustomed to will be provided in a more widely accessible form: online in a new *State of Working America* Web site—both as the tables and charts that traditionally formed the backbone of the previous printed editions as well as being offered in raw form for more data-curious readers to do with what they will. However, in addition to providing the data and analysis, EPI believes that the unique circumstances of today's economy beg for more interpretation, for an articulation of the story behind America's broken economy. This book provides that story.

In *Failure by Design*, Josh Bivens takes an important perspective-clarifying step back from the hundreds of charts in *The State of Working America*, and relates a compelling narrative of our country's economy. The story these charts tell us, he argues, is that our economic system is "human-made," designed by hand, so to speak. These outcomes are subject to improvement going forward as long as different choices are made. Bivens sketches out how policy choices—such as allowing the minimum wage to be eroded by inflation, or tilting the law governing unions and collective bargaining strongly in favor of employers, or crafting rules governing globalization that benefit the already-privileged—have led to the unfortunate outcomes documented in the 20-year history of *The State of Working America*: slow growth of wages and incomes at the bottom and middle coupled with extraordinarily rapid growth at the top. Importantly, Bivens argues that these outcomes were predictable (and predicted), and he provides clear evidence that you do indeed get the economy that you choose.

He also documents that these changes, besides being disadvantageous to rank-and-file American workers, also led to a more fragile economy for everybody. The true danger of this fragility was devastatingly demonstrated by the onset of the Great Recession, when a bubble in real estate, enabled by a financial sector allowed to self-regulate, turned into an economic disaster.

The life-span of *The State of Working America* has seen a consistent movement in the American economy toward less-equal growth, and now, in the aftermath of the Great Recession, Bivens argues that this movement only bought the economy much greater fragility. Bivens' analysis stands firmly on the foundation provided by the work in *The State of Working America*, but it takes a much more pointed policy stand on many of the issues we face. Given the stakes involved in choosing the economy we want as we try to move out of the Great Recession, we thought it was too important to allow the narrative being told in edition after edition to remain buried. *Failure By Design* is our attempt to surface it. We think it is a vital counterpart to the ongoing work of *The State of Working America* series in documenting trends in incomes, wages, employment, and inequality—work that continues at the new Web site and will be resumed in book form in 2012.

The policies that can lead to more durable economic growth that is more broadly shared are not rocket science: a minimum wage that can actually sustain families and that is indexed to keep pace with broader economic growth; labor law reform that allows the 50% of private-sector workers who want to form unions to actually do so without fear of reprisal; trade agreements that extend protections not only to multinational corporations but to America's workers as well; and regulation of the financial sector that made the crucial decisions that turned a housing bubble into a historically bad recession. These are all policies high on the agenda of any progressive. What *Failure by Design* demonstrates, however, is how necessary and how effective a new direction in economic policy making can be. It is not that the economy has been broken for the last 30 years or so, but rather that it is working as it has been designed to work. During this time the reigning economic policy belittled the need for good quality jobs and economic security. In fact, we were told that the various laissez-faire policies pursued—unfettered globalization, deregulation of industries, financial market deregulation, a weakened safety net, and lower labor standards for minimum wages, overtime, discrimination, safety and health, and privatization of public services—would all make us better off as consumers as goods and services became cheaper. It turned out that the predictable deterioration of job quality and greater economic insecurity created an economy that could only grow based on asset bubbles and rising household debt. For 30 years, policy levers have been pulled to help the well-off, and this policy orientation worked spectacularly on its own terms. It's time to change the terms and start using these levers to help everybody.

Lawrence Mishel

Economic Policy Institute president
and author of *The State of Working America* series

The Great Recession
The damage done and the rot revealed

The unemployment rate in the United States stood at 9.6% in August 2010, well over double the rate that prevailed in the same month in 2007, the year before the Great Recession hit. August 2010 also marked the fifth anniversary of Hurricane Katrina making landfall on the Louisiana coast. Drawing parallels between Katrina and the Great Recession may sound like the beginning of an argument for complacency in the face of the worst economic crisis since the Great Depression—after all, you can't change the weather.

But the scale of damage done by Katrina wasn't really about weather but rather the neglect of public goods and social institutions. The rain and wind didn't manage to flood the city—the collapse of levees protecting it did. The weather in the days before the storm didn't prevent residents from evacuating—many simply lacked the means or social networks that would have allowed them to leave as easily as those who could pay for a hotel room or call friends outside the city with extra rooms in their house.

This mirrors many important aspects of the Great Recession. Economic shocks happen—that will never change and is indeed "like the weather." But what determines how much human suffering these shocks leave in their wake is driven by social and political choices about how the economy is managed. It was *not* inevitable that the significant run-up in home prices that began in the late 1990s would end with more than 8 million Americans losing their jobs and unemployment hitting a 25-year peak.

When policy makers failed to rein in a financial sector that was making bets on ever-rising prices, it proved ruinous for the larger economy: poor policy choices amplified what should have been only short-lived over-exuberance among home buyers and sellers into a full-blown economic crisis. In short, a key lesson to be taken both from the aftermath of Katrina and the Great Recession is that blaming simple fate for what has happened absolves those in power far too easily. The scale of casualties of both disasters were determined largely by political choices, not by immutable acts of nature.

Another striking parallel was revealed in the crises' aftermaths. Many Americans following the news coverage of Katrina were shocked to see the depth of poverty that many of their fellow citizens had fallen into. Thousands had been unable to flee the city simply because they lacked a car, money for a hotel room, or friends and family in locales safe from the storm's reach. In the aftermath of the Great Recession, it has become apparent that the neglect of our most vulnerable residents had left them one hard shove away from economic danger or even ruin—living without health insurance, having kids go hungry, evictions, or even flat-out poverty and bankruptcy. At the end of 2007, this hard shove came. This long-term neglect of vulnerable working families was matched only by our solicitude toward the most-privileged: the dismantling of regulations on the financial sector was undertaken with key policy makers voicing confidence that it was "self-regulating" and could be trusted to police itself for the social and economic good of all. Obviously, this was not the case. Ignoring the needs of the most vulnerable and catering to the desires of the most connected surely has nothing to do with the weather, or the market, or any other abstraction outside of our control; it is simply a choice that our political leaders made.

In recent decades, Americans have been presented a number of false choices, false choices presented as gospel, with perhaps the most enduring being the claim that a more fair economy would result in a much less efficient one. There's no evidence to believe this is true—increasing opportunities for those who haven't won life's lottery is as wise an investment for the future as can be made, and too many of the *actual* inefficiencies plaguing our economy are those that put thumbs on the scale for the interests of the well-off.

Unfortunately, the project of decoding these false choices and charting a new economic path has to be started while the U.S. economy remains mired in an economic crisis. While the Great Recession officially ended in the middle of 2009, the nascent recovery is weak and (at the time of this writing) even decelerating. Worse, while the economic freefall of late 2008 and early 2009 temporarily carved out political space to pass ambitious legislation aimed at righting the economic ship—most notably the American Recovery and Reinvestment Act (ARRA)—this political space is quickly getting squeezed by the return of the conventional wisdom that has served working Americans so poorly.

Much remains to be done simply to return the U.S. economy to its far from ideal pre-recession condition. But settling for a simple restoration of the flawed economy we had in 2007 would be a betrayal of American working families. Even during the official economic expansion of the 2000s, the American economy was far from delivering a fair deal for most families. It could have, and should have, done better.

This book aims to provide readers with the evidence they need to evaluate the economic policy choices ahead of us and to demand better outcomes—ensuring a robust recovery from the Great Recession as well as providing a firmer foundation for future growth that can be enjoyed by a much broader range of Americans.

These choices matter—the current precarious state of working America did not come about by happenstance; rather it was the predictable outcome of the political choices made over the preceding three decades. When partisans of the *status quo* tell Americans that there is no alternative or that remorseless economic logic demands our economy look exactly like it has for the past 25 years, they are wrong. The economy that generated sub-par outcomes before the Great Recession and that turned a housing bubble into an economic catastrophe was *designed*. It was designed, specifically, to guarantee that the powerful reaped a larger share of the rewards of overall economic growth. And in this purpose it succeeded.

While it was designed to ensure that the already-rich claimed the lion's share of future growth, it was *marketed* as guaranteeing a more efficient economy for all, so that even as the rich took a larger share, *everybody* would see rising living standards as economic growth accelerated. This marketing campaign turned out to be as reliable as most marketing is in the end: not at all.

A new economic policy that prioritizes rising living standards for the many, not just the few, also demands conscious design. Too many Americans have been told for too long that any tinkering with the current design of the economy would be tantamount to killing the goose that lays the golden eggs. In the aftermath of the Great Recession, the falsity of this claim should be clearer than ever. However, the failure of design in the American economy should have been seen over most of the three decades preceding the Great Recession as well. Income-growth of the vast majority of households lagged far behind overall growth rates, while incomes at the very top swelled to previously unimaginable levels. Growth in living standards could only be purchased by most families through saving less or taking on more debt. The very *definition* of a failing economy should be that most families cannot rely on rising incomes to lift living standards as fast as the overall average. For too long, we have graded the economy on a much more generous curve—whether or not it provided *any growth at all*, regardless of how fast that growth was in historical context or how widely distributed it was.

During this time, it was the work ethic and stoicism of the American people themselves that masked the economy's mismanagement and unequal performance, forestalling an outright crisis. They worked harder and longer and shouldered more debt and more financial insecurity as a means of coping with a radical deceleration in the growth of hourly pay. Finally, even these shock absorbers were completely overwhelmed by economic events when at the end of 2007 a shockwave driven by cluelessness and greed on the part of the country's financial elite broke the economy.

The Great Recession's Trigger

Housing bubble leads to jobs crisis

December 2007 marked the official end of the economic expansion that began in November 2001. The official end of the Great Recession occurred in June 2009, making it the longest recession to hit the U.S. economy since before World War II. This chapter details the damage done since the recession began and the failure of the recovery so far to repair it.

While an increase in housing foreclosures provided the spark, it was the poor economic choices and mismanagement of the previous decade that provided the tinder for the ensuing conflagration. The economic expansion from 2001 to 2007 was among the weakest on record in essentially every way that matters to working Americans. Growth in overall gross domestic product (GDP), workers' salaries and benefits, investment, and employment were the worst of any expansion we have seen since World War II. Typical family incomes grew by *less than half a percent* between 2000 and 2007—*only about one-tenth as fast as the next worst business cycle on record*. From the perspective of America's working families, the economic expansion of the 2000s essentially represented a lost decade of growth.

It didn't have to be that way. Policy makers found plenty of resources to throw at tax cuts aimed disproportionately at corporations and the very rich and at wars abroad. And when partisan politics demanded it, resources were also found to enhance Medicare coverage by adding a prescription drug benefit—but only when bundled with flagrant giveaways to pharmaceutical companies and other corporations. If even a fraction of these resources had found their way into well-targeted interventions to boost the job market, the decade could have been very different, with wage growth supporting living standards instead of debt.

But faster wage growth would, of course, have threatened the only economic indicators that performed above-trend in the 2000s: growth in corporate profits, which during the 2000s saw the fourth-fastest growth of the 10 expansions in the post-war period. These profits were led by the financial sector, which saw its share of overall corporate profits hitting all-time highs. These financial profits were realized largely due to ever-growing returns earned from extending loans to cover the skyrocketing cost of houses, as a bubble in home prices replaced the bubble in stock market prices that had burst in 2001. From 1997 to 2006, inflation-adjusted home prices, which had for decades grown at the typical rate of inflation, nearly doubled.

Besides boosting the bottom line of financial corporations, rising home prices gave American families the chance to borrow against the equity in their houses and give a boost to their living standards, a boost that the broader economy had not afforded them, for example, through rising employment opportunities and wage growth.

And borrow they did—at the height of the housing bubble an amount equal to almost 8% of Americans' total disposable personal income was being extracted from homes. *In short, Americans were using the housing bubble to give themselves the 8% raise that the job market, hampered by anemic growth, was not generating for them.*

Once housing prices stopped rising, however, there was no more equity to extract, and the disadvantage of relying on increasing debt, rather than rising wages, as a means to purchase better living standards became clear.

Millions had been sold mortgages that ballooned in the second or third year, making them unaffordable and requiring those families to seek refinancing. But this refinancing was only possible while rising home prices gave them equity in their homes. With the end of rising housing prices, this game of mortgage hot potato ground to a halt, and millions found themselves stuck with mortgages they couldn't afford or refinance. Just as rising housing prices boosted wealth and spurred economic activity, their decline extinguished wealth and brought the economy to a shuddering halt.

Roughly $8 trillion in housing wealth will likely be erased between the housing market's peak and trough. As American families saw their wealth fading away, they pulled back on their spending—cutting roughly $600 billion in consumer spending from the economy. And the over-building of houses (and corporate real estate) during the bubble meant that this sector contracted by about $600 billion annually as well.

Business investment in equipment and software also collapsed as customers dried up and existing factories and offices went idle. During the depth of the financial crisis, firms were threatened with difficulty just maintaining the cash and credit flows needed to keep their operations running.

That the 2000s economy depended on an unsustainable housing bubble is painfully obvious in retrospect and was actually pointed out in real time by many. What is less clear is what we as a society will learn from this episode to guide future choices. Many have tried to make the case that the root of the problem was some moral shortcoming of Americans—instead of waiting to earn the money to consume the better things in life they took an irresponsible short-cut that was bound to end in catastrophe.

This view should be soundly rejected. Was it unwise for American households to take on more debt to buy homes that would end up worth less than what was paid for them? Of course. But did the economic policy-making elite or the chattering class try to warn them about this as it unfolded? To the contrary, economic elites either ignored or even sneered at anyone warning of a housing bubble; and the most elite of all, Alan Greenspan, the legendarily influential chairman of the Federal Reserve, actually counseled in 2004 for potential homebuyers to take on more debt with less stable interest rates in order to be able to afford even more expensive houses. Furthermore, the notion that today's Americans are less patient than their forebears is hard to square with the fact that typical family incomes and living standards have grown (even with the fuel of the housing bubble) at just a fraction of the pace that characterized the economies that their parents and grandparents grew up in.

The moral of the 2000s economy has little to do with the typical American's "character" and much to do with how the economy is managed, specifically the choices regarding who reaps the economy's fruits. When the financial sector wanted to roll back regulations to enable them to extend even riskier loans, which led to the disasterous housing bubble, the regulators gave in. This was a policy decision with consequences beyond the financial sector. When this sector also benefited from a flood of cheap loans from abroad that resulted in the dollar rising to levels that ruined the prospects for U.S. manufacturers, their desire to keep the foreign spigots on trumped the pleas from manufacturing companies and workers to stem the flow. And when the 2001 recession was accompanied by the longest jobless recovery in history, instead of funding investments in safety nets and infrastructure that would have boosted the job market and quickly reduced unemployment, we got tax cuts that disproportionately benefited the already affluent. Again, a policy choice with distinct economic consequences was made.

In short, the anemic expansion from 2001 to 2007 was founded on an unsustainable housing bubble, but this bubble was allowed to swell to disastrous proportions because policy makers chose to allow it. The resulting Great Recession should make fully clear that *nothing about economic outcomes is pre-ordained*. Our leaders failed to make the tough choices in favor of the American people and instead sided with the rich and powerful. This led the economy to ruin.

As we move forward, it is time to remember how important these choices are. The rest of this section details the damage done by the Great Recession. Sections that follow will show how the previous 30 years of economic mismanagement resulted in a cracked foundation that was unable to withstand the economic shock that led to the Great Recession.

Fallout: the job market

By now, most know that the Great Recession resulted in shocking amounts of job loss. What is perhaps less well-known is just how historically large the job loss and concomitant rise in the unemployment rate have been. Another disturbing feature of the Great Recession is that it follows two recessions in which the recovery in jobs was painfully slow relative to the post-World War II norm. If recovery from the Great Recession continues this pattern, the sheer size of the resultant jobs gap means that *it could well be a decade or more before the pre-recession unemployment rate is restored* unless policy makers take much more aggressive steps to jumpstart this recovery.

While the Great Recession was in many ways a broad-based catastrophe, affecting all racial and socioeconomic groups adversely, it continued the familiar pattern of inflicting the most damage on those who were most vulnerable and had been suffering the most even before the recession. For example, the unemployment rate for African Americans has risen more than 50% faster than the rate for white workers, and incomes for typical African American families have fallen much further between 2007 and 2009 than incomes for white families.

FIGURE 1

Recession has left in its wake a job shortfall of 11 million
Payroll employment and the number of jobs needed to keep up with the growth in working-age population

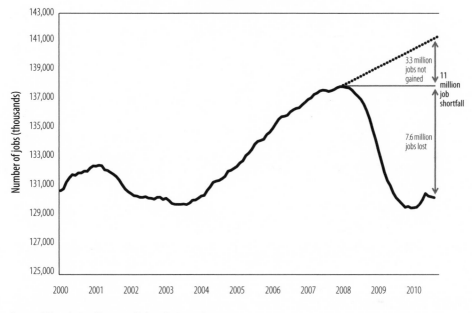

Source: EPI analysis of Bureau of Labor Statistics data.

Figure 1: This chart shows total payroll employment from 2000 until August 2010. Besides the 7.6 million jobs lost during the Great Recession, the dotted trend line reflects the fact that to keep the unemployment rate stable the economy needs to create more than 100,000 jobs per month just to keep pace with growth in the working-age population. Getting the job market back to its pre-recession health will thus require 11 million jobs—7.6 million jobs lost plus 3.3 million jobs needed for new labor market entrants.

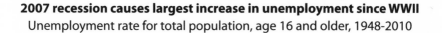

2007 recession causes largest increase in unemployment since WWII
Unemployment rate for total population, age 16 and older, 1948-2010

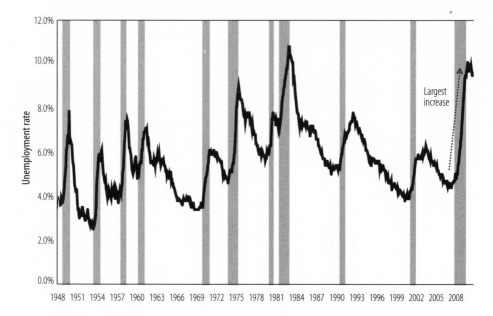

Note: Shaded areas denote recession.

Source: Bureau of Labor Statistics, Current Population Survey.

Figure 2: Unemployment has soared during the Great Recession. It reached a 26-year peak in 2009, and the increase over the pre-recession rate is the largest since the Great Depression.

FIGURE 3

A more comprehensive measure of slack in the labor market
The number of underemployed workers, including those unemployed,
part-time for economic reasons, and marginally attached, 1994 - 2010

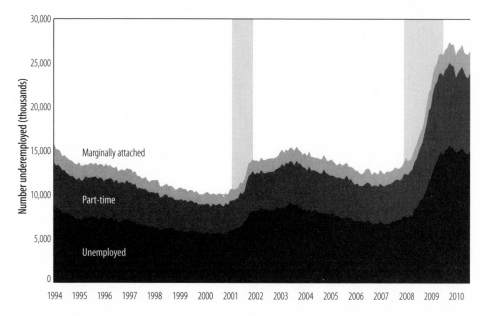

Note: Shaded areas denote recession.

Source: Bureau of Labor Statistics, Current Population Survey.

Figure 3: The unemployment rate by itself masks important dimensions of labor market distress. Besides the jobless, the Great Recession has resulted in a very large rise in workers who would prefer full-time work but can only find part-time jobs and jobless people who are willing and available to work but are not formally classified as unemployed because they are not actively seeking jobs. In short, the underemployment rate has risen in lock-step with the unemployment rate.

FIGURE 4

Not enough jobs for too many people
The job seekers ratio (the number of unemployed workers per every job opening)

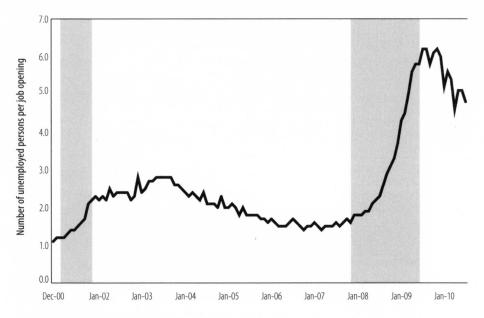

Note: Shaded areas denote recession.

Source: EPI analysis of Bureau of Labor Statistics data.

Figure 4: Why is it so hard to find work? Because in August 2010 there were roughly five unemployed workers for every job opening in the economy. To be clear—these are actual unemployed workers, not applicants. There could well be dozens of applicants for each opening as each unemployed worker may send out multiple applications.

FIGURE 5

Jobs fall further and longer
Indexed job loss for four recessions

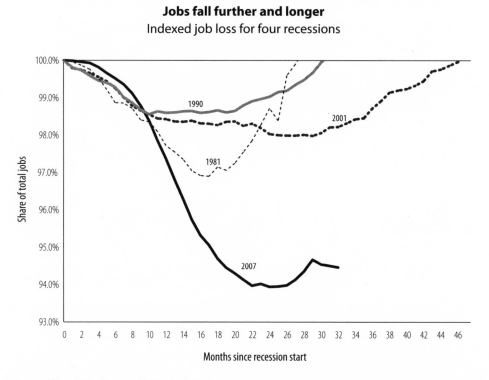

Source: EPI analysis of Bureau of Labor Statistics data.

Figure 5: The scale of job loss in the Great Recession dwarfs that of previous recessions.

FIGURE 6

What will recovery look like?
Three possible paths to recovery: following the path
of recoveries in the '80s, '90s, and 2000s

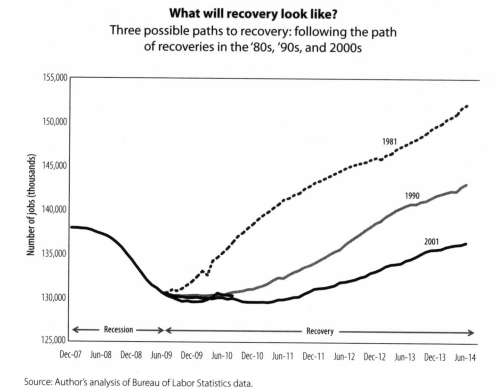

Source: Author's analysis of Bureau of Labor Statistics data.

Figure 6: Like the previous two recessions, the current recession has been characterized by very slow labor market recoveries. If jobs are added only at the pace that
characterized the recoveries of the early 1990s and early 2000s, because of the much
greater scale of job loss in the Great Recession it could be well into the next decade
before we regain all the lost jobs.

FIGURE 7

Always an unemployment emergency for some
Unemployment rates by race, 1972-present

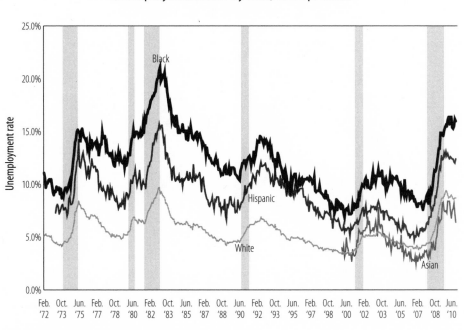

Source: Author's analysis of Bureau of Labor Statistics data.

Figure 7: The full complement (53 weeks worth) of "emergency" unemployment compensation has been automatically triggered in the Great Recession in states where the overall unemployment rate exceeded 8.5%. However, the unemployment rate for African Americans has been lower than 8.5% for only 45 of the 369 months since 1979, or roughly 12% of the time.

FIGURE 8

Unequal burden of income loss over the Great Recession
Change in real median household income, by race and ethnicity,
2007-08 and 2008-09

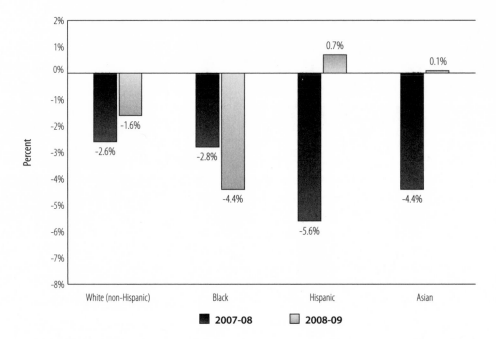

Source: Author's analysis of U.S. Census Bureau data.

Figure 8: Income losses for the median African American family since the Great Recession began have been roughly twice as large in percentage terms as those for white families.

Fallout: broader measures of economic security— poverty, health insurance, and net wealth

The failures in the job market both cause and exacerbate economic insecurity. The loss of jobs, the cutback of hours, and the reduced bargaining power of workers have led to a sharp increase in those living in poverty and going without health insurance. Falling household incomes also mean a sharp reduction in the typical nest-egg accumulated by families over the past decade. All of this has made economic life much more insecure for America's working families.

This erosion of security follows a weak expansion that saw few, if any, durable gains made in any of these areas. (The gains in typical families' net worth during the 2000s were overwhelmingly driven by the housing bubble and have largely been erased now.) The poverty rate and the share of those without employer-provided health insurance actually rose *during the expansion*. Family incomes were essentially flat. In short, by these measures it already seemed like a lost decade of economic growth for many Americans. The Great Recession all but ensures that the coming decade will also be devoid of progress for working families.

FIGURE 9

Another casualty of the Great Recession—rising poverty

The percentage-point increase in the poverty rate following business cycle peak to height of poverty, working-age population, five recessions*

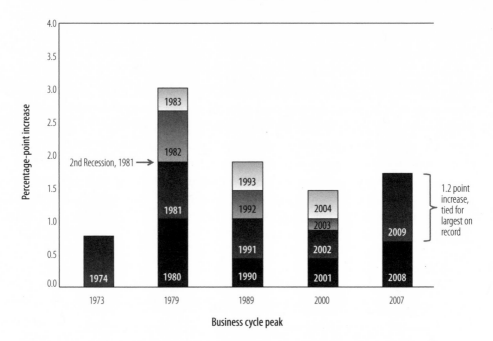

* The data labels show the total increase in poverty, from the business cycle peak to the poverty peak, and the year in which it was reached. For the current downturn, poverty is projected to rise until 2011. The largest increase, 1979-1983, occured over two recessions, one in 1980 and the second in 1981.

Source: EPI analysis of U.S. Census Bureau data.

Figure 9: Poverty predictably rises as the labor market deteriorates. The increase in poverty among the working age population that has occurred since the start of the Great Recession ties for the largest on record.

FIGURE 10

Health coverage erodes, slowly and then quickly
Rates of health insurance coverage, under-65 population, 2000-10

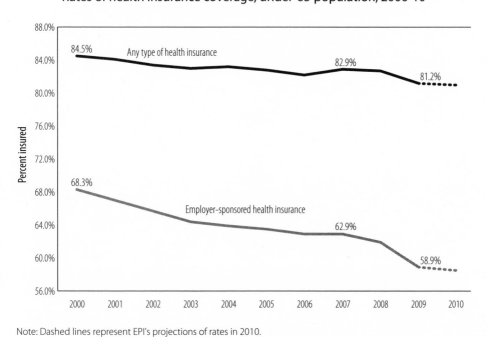

Note: Dashed lines represent EPI's projections of rates in 2010.

Source: Author's analysis of the Current Population Survey, Annual Social and Economic Supplement.

Figure 10: Employer-sponsored insurance was eroding even during the weak economic expansion of the 2000s. This erosion became a landslide in 2009. While public insurance expansions took up some of the slack, falling job-based coverage led to large overall declines in coverage as well.

FIGURE 11

Household wealth declines
Median net worth* of households by race, 2001-09

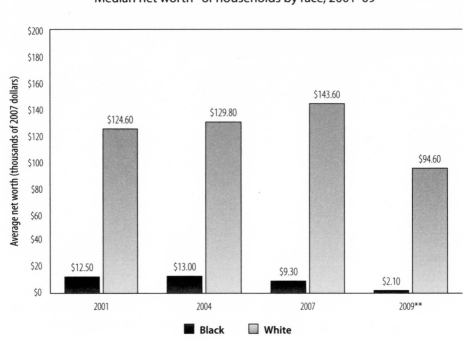

* Net worth is defined as total assets less total liabilities.
** 2009 data are estimated based on asset changes from the Federal Reserve Flow of Funds data.
Source: EPI (Wolff) analysis of Survey of Consumer Finances data.

Figure 11: The bursting housing bubble led to sharp reversal in net worth for American families.

The Policy Response to the Great Recession

What was done and did it work?

While the official beginning of the Great Recession is the first month of 2008, the first defensive actions traditionally taken to fight recessions—cuts in the short-term interest rate controlled by the Federal Reserve—were already well underway by then. As the first ripples of the housing bubble's burst were felt in the financial sector, the Federal Reserve (exquisitely sensitive to the needs of banks and financial institutions) had begun aggressively cutting rates months before.

The rationale behind interest rate cuts is that cheaper debt will spur families to buy more houses and durable goods (like cars) that require financing and will also induce businesses to borrow to undertake increased investment in plants and equipment.

However, falling home prices meant that even interest rate cuts were unlikely to convince households to buy into the housing market, nullifying a key channel through which the Federal Reserve can boost the economy. Worse, cuts to short-term interest rates have a limit—they cannot fall below zero; who would pay a bank to hold their money for them when they could just buy a safe? Interest rates ran up against these limits early on while the economy continued to spiral downward.

Job loss accelerated at a terrifying rate in late 2008. In November, December, and January 2009—roughly between the election and the inauguration of President Barack Obama—more than 2 million jobs were lost. The worsening crisis led to the formation and passage of the American Recovery and Reinvestment Act, or simply the Recovery Act. Since its passage, the Recovery Act has been a focus of much controversy.

In fact, the theory behind the Recovery Act is basic economics, but a kind that does not always make intuitive sense to many. As private households and businesses reduce their spending and try to work off their overhang of debt, the only way to keep unemployment from spiking is to have the public sector fill the gap by increasing its debt and using it to finance spending on safety net programs, investments, or tax cuts. Increasing *public* debt to cushion the economic shock of falling *private* debt might sound wrong to many, but it's not. It is the only way to push back against rising unemployment until the private sector has paid down enough of its debt to begin spending again.

The dynamics of the Great Recession

The specific problems stemming from the bursting of the housing bubble are (a) with less wealth, households have pulled back on spending, (b) after overbuilding, home builders have radically downsized, and (c) because of (a) and (b), future customers are scarce so businesses have cut back investments in plants and equipment. All of these things undermine demand for goods and services in the economy, and this fall-off in demand for economic output means that demand for *workers* falls in turn, leading to job loss and a spike in the unemployment rate.

To ensure that demand doesn't remain so low that it worsens unemployment requires finding a replacement for the consumer and business spending that was extinguished by the bursting of the housing bubble.

Increasing exports could in theory have been such a replacement, but given the huge size of the U.S. economy, the fact that most of what is produced and consumed here is still domestically made, and that the Great Recession had spread globally, there just weren't enough foreign consumers to plausibly allow exports alone to pull the economy out of recession. This crosses off three recession-fighting strategies from the list: increases in purchasing power fueled by consumers, by businesses, and via exports. This leaves increasing purchasing power fueled by public funds. And since we don't want to neutralize the demand-generating impact of this public purchasing power by raising taxes (which shrink private disposable income, the precise opposite of what is needed), this public expenditure should be financed *by debt*.

The public funds should be well-targeted: tax cuts and government transfers (unemployment insurance, food stamps, payments to Social Security beneficiaries, Medicaid and Medicare) should go to those most likely to spend the money quickly, and direct government spending should go to those projects that will both create jobs in the short term and make us more productive for the long term. But, in the end, what works to end recessions that prove immune to conventional actions by the Federal Reserve is a public sector that leans against the headwind of reduced private spending by increasing its own spending.

It is clear that this works. Macroeconomic researchers at Goldman Sachs have noted that the shock to private sector spending caused by the bursting of the housing bubble is actually *larger* than the shock that led to the Great Depression. However, because falling incomes also led to falling tax collections, and because falling incomes and joblessness led to automatic increases in safety net programs like unemployment insurance and food stamps and Medicaid, this led to a purely *mechanical* increase in the federal budget deficit of roughly three-quarters of a *trillion* dollars. These automatic tax reductions and transfer payments buoyed private households' disposable incomes and acted as a powerful shock absorber against the damage wrought by the bursting housing bubble.

One testament to the fact that rising budget deficits act as a shock absorber against collapsing private-sector spending is the fact that essentially *no* professional economist criticized the increase in the budget deficit that arose before the passage of the Recovery Act; one can find almost nobody arguing that policy should have kept the budget deficit from rising between January 2008 and February 2009.

The Recovery Act represented the correct assessment by policy makers that the shock absorption provided by the purely *mechanical* rise in the deficit was not sufficient, even when paired with the interest rate cuts undertaken by the Federal Reserve. So, policy makers rightly aimed to provide an even larger cushion to the economy with the Recovery Act. Despite being premised on exactly the same theory as the rationale for automatic stabilizers, because it had a clear political sponsor (the Obama administration), the Recovery Act became flypaper for criticism of all kinds.

Recovery Act controversies: what was in it?

One controversy surrounding the Recovery Act concerns the composition of the Act, with many critics arguing that it was too heavily weighted toward spending at the expense of tax cuts to stimulate the economy. However, less than 15% of the Act's appropriations have actually funded direct government spending. More than a third of the appropriations were for tax cuts, while the remainder went to transfer payments to individuals and states.

Besides simply being wrong, this criticism is ironic given that most macroeconomic research indicates that increasing the debt to pay for tax cuts is a *less* efficient way to generate output and jobs than direct government spending. Compounding this irony, the tax cuts preferred by many of the Act's critics—those going to businesses—were far and away *the least effective* stimulus included in the Act. Tax cuts are less efficient job creators (especially those not targeted to lower-income households) because they may be saved instead of spent, and because many of the business tax cuts were essentially windfalls (often retroactive), rewarding activity that would have been done (or had actually already happened) even without the Act.

FIGURE 12

What was in the Recovery Act?
(Billions of dollars)

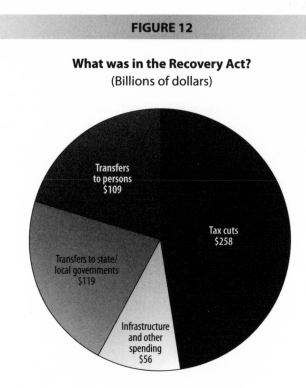

Transfers
to persons
$109

Tax cuts
$258

Transfers to state/
local governments
$119

Infrastructure
and other
spending
$56

Source: Blinder and Zandi (2010).

Figure 12: Contrary to most impressions, tax cuts were the single-largest category of the Recovery Act and infrastructure spending was less than 15% of the package.

On the other hand, safety net programs—such as unemployment insurance, nutrition assistance, and health insurance supports—are by definition *well-targeted*: they go to those families whose incomes have fallen below a threshold or who have recently suffered job loss. Consequently, recipients are much more likely to spend these payments—they have to. And in terms of making sure that all increases in public debt are spent, infrastructure spending is best of all—none of it can be saved; it all must be spent.

In essence, if Congress had included more tax cuts aimed at high-income households and businesses, the effectiveness of the Recovery Act would have been seriously reduced. Given that the next criticism of the Recovery Act argues that it was ineffective, it is more than ironic that these two arguments ("more tax cuts, more effective") generally get peddled by the same critic within the space of a couple of sentences.

Recovery Act controversies: did it work at all?

Most of the controversy surrounding the Act concerns whether or not it helped at all to stabilize economic output and create or save jobs.

A facile debate technique used by those contending that the Recovery Act did nothing invokes the Obama administration's (admittedly ill-advised) forecast that the unemployment rate would rise to roughly 9% if the Recovery Act was not passed and would not reach 8% if it was enacted. When unemployment peaked at 10.1% *after* its passage, many critics pounced, sometimes going as far as to claim that it had even somehow made things worse.

The problem with this interpretation is that it fails to consider the fact that it was not the Recovery Act that failed, but rather the imagination of economic forecasters (both within as well as outside the Obama administration) about how much damage the collapsing housing bubble would do to the economy. In short, the difference between an economy with and without the Recovery Act has come in just as advertised: *the economy has between 3 to 4 million jobs more than it would have had if the Act had not passed.*

FIGURE 13

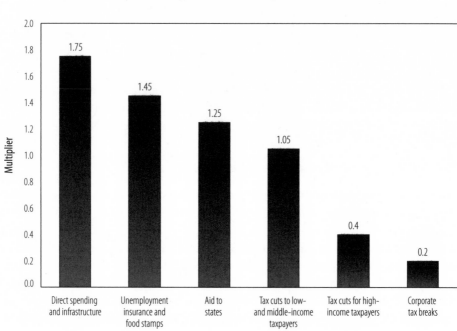

What is the most effective stimulus?
"Bang-for-buck" multipliers*

* Measures total increase in economic activity associated with a $1 increase in the deficit.
Source: Congressional Budget Office data.

Figure 13: Economic forecasters agree that direct spending and safety net supports are the most effective kinds of economic stimulus, while tax cuts to the well-off and to business are the least effective.

FIGURE 14

Quarterly change in real GDP, consumption expenditures, and employment

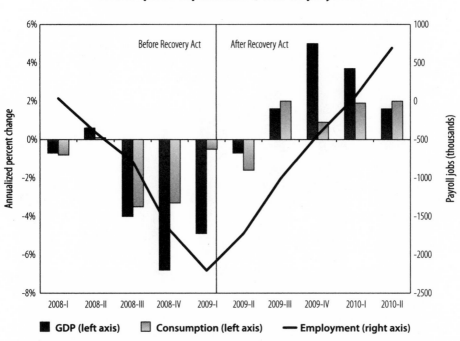

Source: EPI analysis of Bureau of Labor Statistics data and Bureau of Economic Analysis data.

Figure 14: Growth in GDP, consumer spending, and overall employment jump up markedly when Recovery Act spending takes effect in the second quarter of 2009.

FIGURE 15

Contribution of Recovery Act to GDP by the second quarter of 2010

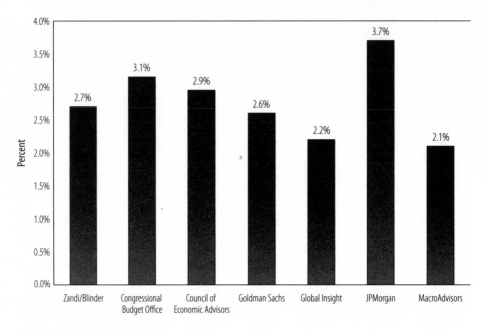

Source: Data from sources listed above.

Figure 15: Among those who get paid to forecast where the economy will be quarter-to-quarter and to know what drives changes, there is a consensus that the Recovery Act added markedly to economic growth.

FIGURE 16

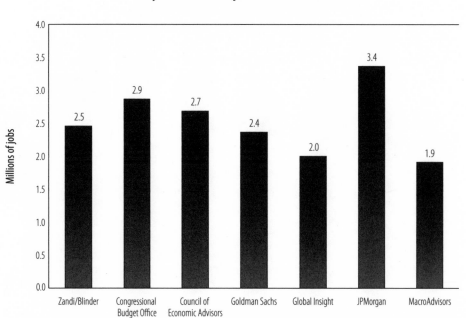

Contribution of Recovery Act to employment by the second quarter of 2010

Source: Data from sources listed above.

Figure 16: The economic growth generated by the Recovery Act supported job growth, leading to millions of workers having jobs because of the Act.

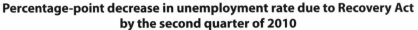

FIGURE 17

Percentage-point decrease in unemployment rate due to Recovery Act by the second quarter of 2010

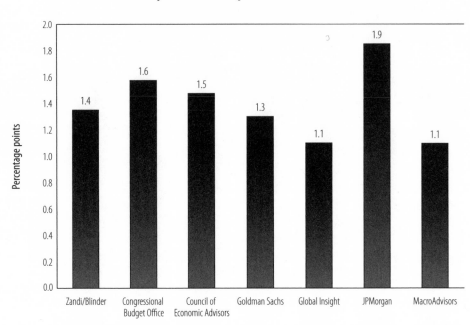

Source: Data from sources listed above.

Figure 17: New jobs created by the Recovery Act kept the unemployment rate from rising even further than it did.

The underlying trend of the economy, however, was far worse than most forecast. The unemployment rate without the Recovery Act would have reached nearly 12%, not the 9% foreseen by the Obama administration.

A good metaphor for this controversy is the temperature in a log cabin on a cold winter's night. Say that the weather forecast is for the temperature to reach 30 degrees Fahrenheit. To stay warm, you decide to burn three logs in the fireplace. You do the math (and chemistry) and calculate that burning these three logs will generate enough heat to bring the inside of the cabin to 50 degrees, or 20 degrees warmer than the ambient temperature.

But the forecast is wrong—and instead temperatures plummet to 10 degrees outside and burning the logs only results in a cabin temperature of 30 degrees. Has log burning failed as a strategy to generate heat? Of course not. Has your estimate of the effectiveness of log burning been wildly wrong? Nope—it was exactly right—it added 20 degrees to the ambient temperature. The only lesson from this is a simple one: since the weather turned out worse than expected, you need more logs.

What is often unappreciated in public debate is that this perspective—that the economy needed more, not less stimulus—is the essential consensus among economic forecasters, both private and public. It is also the consensus that the Recovery Act largely worked as advertised—creating or saving 3-4 million jobs by June 2010. In short, for those whose salary depends on knowing what moves the economy from quarter to quarter, there is unanimity that the Act saved or created millions of jobs.

Recovery Act controversies: why has consumer and not government spending led the recovery?

Another common criticism of the Recovery Act is that because the recovery has mostly been led by a rebound of consumer spending, and not by federal government spending, then the Recovery Act *cannot* be the source of recovery. A related criticism looks at the direct spending tracked by the Recovery.gov reporting system and points to the fact that fewer than a million jobs have been linked to the Recovery Act.

These criticisms fail to understand the components of the Act. Again, the lion's share of Recovery Act spending actually financed tax cuts and transfers straight to households, not direct government spending. Since the single largest component of Recovery Act spending was tax cuts and transfers to individuals, it is here that the Recovery Act's "footprint" should be the largest if it was effective; and this is exactly where it *is* the largest.

A proxy for market-based incomes (known as personal income minus transfers) cratered during the Great Recession, falling by more than in any previous recession. Yet, disposable income (i.e., the income that households actually have available to spend) held up well and was actually *higher* in June 2010 than at the beginning of the recession. This was made possible by the tax cuts and transfer payments (both those that kick in automatically as well as those that were part of the Recovery Act) taking effect during the recession and through 2009. In short, this support of *private* spending is the predictable outcome of slanting the Recovery Act so far toward tax cuts and safety net spending.

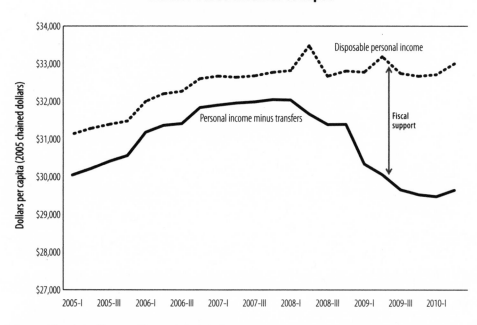

FIGURE 18

**Recovery Act keeps spending power up even as
market-based incomes collapse**

Source: EPI analysis of Bureau of Economic Analysis data.

Figure 18: Contrary to most impressions, the primary "footprint" of the Recovery Act should be seen in higher disposable incomes for households, not in increased government spending. This chart shows that as market incomes fell **(personal incomes minus transfers)** the resources available for households to spend **(personal disposable income)** actually held up well over the course of the recession, buoyed by both tax cuts and transfer payments in the Recovery Act.

The Great Recession Ended More Than a Year Ago— so, "Mission Accomplished"?

The official recovery from the Great Recession began in the middle of 2009. So, is the work of policy makers done?

Not by a long shot.

The Recovery Act stopped the downward spiral, but unless further action is taken to spur job growth, then the unemployment rate is likely to hover between 9.5% and 10% for the next year, making it two straight years at this elevated level. This extended period of high unemployment will continue to inflict great damage and cause insecurity among America's working families. Wages, incomes, poverty, and health insurance coverage all moved in the wrong direction following the sharp rise in unemployment caused by the Great Recession. Unless there is a rapid reversal there will be little improvement in any of these. Worse, if unemployment remains high for too long, permanent scars will develop—lifetime earnings will be lower, people will fall into poverty traps, and the formative years of children's lives will be marked by stress, frequent moves between schools that impede learning, and less consistent access to health care.

Apathy, not overreach

In short, the one *valid* criticism of what has been done so far by policy makers is not that it constitutes overreach, but in fact that *it is not nearly enough*. While the initial actions of the Federal Reserve and the passage of the Recovery Act were serious responses to events occurring in real time, it has since become crystal clear that they were still not enough to bring the economy quickly back to health. For some reason, however, because the policy responses to the Great Recession were (by some measures) larger than during previous recessions, there is great reluctance to do more. But the Great Recession is far larger than previous recessions, so "larger than what we've done before" is a strange benchmark to apply. Imagine water overtopping a levy built to contain a flood. Some begin arguing that more sandbags should be filled to add height to the levy. Others argue "but this is the tallest levy we've ever built, so we should stop." Which approach makes more sense?

Going forward, building a taller levy requires a combination of more aggressive fiscal policy support, exchange rate policy that allows us to narrow the trade deficit and keep demand from leaking abroad to our trading partners, and a Federal Reserve that goes far beyond its traditional remedy of lowering short-term interest rates to more aggressively providing monetary stimulus to the economy. This combination of policies should be continued *until the economy recovers*. However, it is clear to anybody who has followed economic policy making in recent decades that each of these maneuvers would represent a substantial break from the orthodoxy that has prevailed during the past 30 years. These political and ideological barriers to sound economic policy are inflicting a huge cost today. Over the past three decades, many of the bad economic choices that once were hotly contested have become so ossified that they have become a seemingly permanent part of the economic landscape. This has kept the economy from reaching its potential for working families. There is a danger that these failed policies will be perpetuated even today—already key policy makers seem by their actions to have thrown up their hands and declared nothing can be done to push down the 9.6% unemployment rate. If this complacency is not contested, then tolerance of extremely high unemployment will quickly become the "new normal."

Exchange rate policy

It is clear by now that the chronic trade deficit is a problem for the U.S. economy. The cause of this deficit is simply that the U.S. dollar is priced too high in world markets— U.S. exports are too expensive for trade partners, foreign imports are too cheap for U.S. consumers, and, as a result, imports greatly exceed exports.

Often in such situations, market forces will tend to push an overvalued dollar back down to a more sustainable level. However, this adjustment is currently being impeded by the decision of several of our most important trade partners (notably China) to spend hundreds of billions of dollars each year to buy dollar-denominated assets, leading to an increase in the demand for, and thus the price of, dollars. During the boom years, the pros and cons of this odd economic relationship—one in which much poorer trading partners lent us hundreds of billions of dollars each year—were less clear. The drain on demand for U.S.-produced goods and services was counter-balanced to some degree by the downward pressure on interest rates provided by the foreign money flowing into the country. But now, the U.S. economy is getting no boost from lower interest rates and the huge increase in domestic savings has satisfied all new demands for debt. Yet the downside of the overvalued dollar remains: the United States exports too little and imports too much.

Engineering a decline in foreign purchase of dollar-denominated assets and allowing the dollar to decline during a period of high unemployment and low interest rates would provide a valuable stimulus to U.S. jobs. Yet, because for decades the elite consensus on trade was that it must remain resolutely unmanaged, or at least unmanaged by us (it is currently being actively managed by our trade partners), this avenue for stimulus remains unexplored.

Monetary policy

A similar adherence to orthodoxy hamstrings prospects for using monetary policy to spur job growth going forward. The traditional tool that the Federal Reserve uses to fight recessions is lowering short-term interest rates, which it controls directly (i.e., rates at which banks lend to each other and at which the Fed will loan directly to banks). The Fed hopes that by lowering these short-term rates, arbitrage will lead to a reduction in the longer-term rates that affect businesses' decisions to borrow to build new factories and purchase new equipment as well as families' decisions to borrow to buy things like houses and cars.

These short-term rates currently sit essentially at zero, and yet the economy flounders. However, the Fed does have other tools. As emphasized in the past research of current Fed Chair Ben Bernanke, the Fed could, for example, buy long-term debt and hence drive down long-term interest rates more directly—either on U.S. government debt or even more promisingly on private-sector debt. This could directly lower the relevant costs of borrowing in the private sector for businesses and households.

Additionally, the Fed could publicly announce that it will target a higher rate of inflation, which could help erode the huge overhang of private-sector debt that is still keeping households and firms from undertaking new spending. All of these things, again, would fly in the face of orthodoxy that has governed the U.S. economy in recent decades. And yet all of these would help spur job growth. Pushing down interest rates on long-term (especially private) debt could encourage businesses and households to start spending again on new investment projects, real estate, and those consumer goods that require borrowing to buy. A higher rate of inflation would erode some of the debt hanging over household and business balance sheets. One reason why so many think homes are a great investment is that for a time between the late 1960s and early 1980s, inflation quickly eroded the value of many mortgage holders' debt.

Fiscal policy

Perhaps the most puzzling reticence among policy makers today is their failure to use further fiscal policy measures (i.e., something like another Recovery Act) to target a lower rate of unemployment. Given the successes of the Recovery Act (documented previously) and given that many of the potential downsides of fiscal expansion have clearly not materialized, politics alone seems to be in the way of using fiscal policy to spur economic activity.

The most-cited *economic* downside of larger federal budget deficits is the fear that, as the government competes with private borrowers for savings, interest rates will spike and private-sector investment will be "crowded out." However, this argument does not hold for an economy where households and private business are trying to vastly increase their savings, not take on more debt. In this case, there is no competition for scarce savings, and there is no upward pressure on interest rates. This means that there is no danger that private investment will be crowded out. Indeed, because the biggest determinant of firms' investment decisions is their assessment of sales growth, the Recovery Act, by supporting household purchasing power and salvaging potential customers for businesses, has surely crowded *in* business investment that otherwise would have sagged even more.

The evidence firmly supports this sanguine view of interest rates—rates on 30-year bonds are far lower than before the recession began and have actually fallen since the passage of the Recovery Act. Clearly there are very few competitors to the federal government in looking to increase debt, hence interest rate pressure is non-existent.

Yet fear (even hysteria) of larger deficits is constantly presented as the trump card against those arguing for more fiscal support for the economy. Given that there's no economic merit to this argument, and given that fears of deficits have done little to derail proposals to lessen tax rates on the affluent, its durability seems rooted in the odd Beltway ideology that simply objects to using public spending to ease Americans' economic worries.

Clear economics, fuzzy politics

Can we be absolutely sure that more support to the economy (through fiscal, exchange, or monetary policies) will translate into a lower unemployment rate and better prospects for finding jobs? Yes, absolutely. For all the talk about "jobless recoveries" and hand-wringing over what causes them, one thing is perfectly clear: faster overall growth translates into lower unemployment, and the cause of past jobless recoveries is simply slower-than-average growth.

The good news is that we know how to spur this growth—the simplest path is for the federal government to spend more and/or tax less as long as unemployment remains high. *The government also needs to tolerate the resulting deficits to whatever degree it takes to get the job done.* The better news is that the fiscal costs of these deficits are at historic lows: the recession has driven the costs of borrowing to record lows. A similar strategy is needed for monetary and exchange rate policies—more aggressive measures need to be pursued, as the costs of these policies are minimal in a depressed economy.

The bad news is simply that too many policy makers have either not absorbed these economic truths or they simply object to upsetting the economic strategy that has paid off well for their most-privileged constituents for decades. Until they can be convinced, either of these economic truths or the political rightness of sharing economic opportunity with a larger group, the prospects for an economic recovery are dim. Convincing some of them will require that they jettison a cherished idea that has gripped too many in the policy-making elite over the past three decades: deficits are always and everywhere bad, and a smaller deficit is always a worthy policy target in and of itself. Convincing the others requires that they recognize the economic plight of those who don't contribute to their campaigns. As the next section of this book makes clear, this is just one plank of the dominant economic strategy of the past 30 years that must be replaced. But we should be clear about this—until we change our policy course and affirmatively decide to design a different economy, we will not get different results. Not for nothing did Albert Einstein define insanity as "doing the same thing over and over again but expecting different results."

This adherence to economic doctrine, even in the face of clear evidence that it is ill-serving to the interests of most Americans, should be no surprise to those who have followed the U.S. economy in the past 30 years. For decades, policies that promised to spur growth and raise living standards have failed to deliver for typical Americans but have provided previously unimagined wealth for the most privileged slice of the American economy. Yet despite their failure to deliver the goods for most American families, there has been no move to re-assess them. And this failure to challenge the Washington policy orthodoxy is, sadly, one thing that the Great Recession has so far not changed.

FIGURE 19

Fast growth, falling unemployment; slow growth, rising unemployment
Eight-quarter change in GDP growth and unemployment, 1983-present

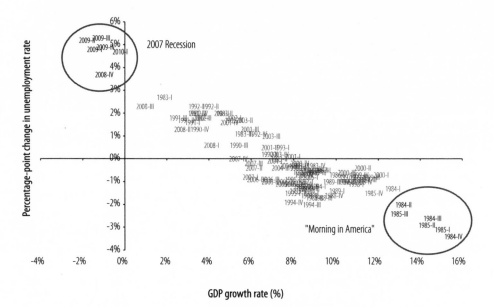

Source: EPI analysis of Bureau of Economic Analysis and Bureau of Labor Statistics data.

Figure 19: It is no mystery what causes job growth: fast growth in economic output leads to fast growth in jobs, period. Getting serious about creating jobs means spurring economic growth. The very rapid improvement in the unemployment rate following the 1982 peak was no mystery—it was simply driven by very rapid overall economic growth.

The Cracked Foundation
Revealed by the
Great Recession

J ust as Hurricane Katrina revealed underlying weaknesses in the physical, economic, and social infrastructure of New Orleans, the Great Recession has revealed similar weaknesses in the overall American economy.

In the quarter-century following World War II, economic growth in the United States was rapid and equitably distributed. To be sure, social and economic inequalities were rife, but the trajectory for the typical American family was steady economic progress. Beginning in the late 1970s, this trajectory flattened as wage growth slowed to a crawl. Any increases in the typical families' living standards thereafter were essentially bought through increased working time and less savings.

The past 30 years has seen a number of important trends that were the result of specific policy decisions: the consistent erosion of the minimum wage's purchasing power; a rapid decline in the power of organized labor; a rapid increase in the share of the U.S. economy that has been exposed to global competition; a dismantling of regulations that governed the financial sector; and a shift to monetary and fiscal policies that favor budget balance and low rates of inflation over the insurance of full employment. All of these shifts have, predictably, battered the bargaining power of typical American workers to the benefit of our society's most privileged.

Falling minimum wage

In 1968, the inflation-adjusted value of the minimum wage was $8.54 in 2009 dollars. For almost the next 40 years, its value marched downward, arrested only occasionally by Congressional action. By 2006, after nearly a decade without a raise, this value had fallen to $5.48, the lowest on record. Raises since 2006 pushed its value back up to $7.25, still far short of the value that prevailed 40 years ago—and this in an economy that had seen economic output per worker rise by almost 80% in those 40 years.

Assault on workers' right to organize

In 1973, roughly a quarter of private-sector workers belonged to a union (and slightly more were covered by a union contract). By 2007, this coverage had fallen by two-thirds to 7.5%. While some of this fall could be attributed to a changing economy— especially a unionized manufacturing sector that was shrinking as a share of the total economy—most of the decline was due to increased employer aggressiveness in fighting unions. This can be seen by contrasting this fall in private-sector unionization with the sharp increase in public-sector union coverage. Public employers are generally barred from fighting unionization drives as aggressively as private-sector employers.

Given this more neutral setting, workers in this sector have chosen to unionize in greater numbers in recent decades. And much research indicates that the *desire* for unionization is as strong as ever (or stronger) among American workers, yet employer intransigence keeps this increased desire from translating into new union members.

Global integration for America's workers and insulation for elites

A key factor in the decline of private-sector unionization, especially in the manufacturing sector, has been the growing openness of the American economy to global competition. The possibility of implicitly replacing American workers with imports has shifted bargaining power away from these workers and has directly stunted wage growth as well as made it harder to unionize. While the rise of globalization has been facilitated by technology and policy decisions made abroad, the consensus of economic elites in the United States has been to accommodate and accelerate the integration of the U.S. and global economies—or at least to integrate their labor markets so that rank-and-file American workers must compete with the rest of the world. The result has been a predictable leveling of the wages of these American workers. Conversely, those workers and capital owners that were shielded from the downsides of global competition have seen their incomes soar.

The rise of finance

A large share of those individuals who have seen their incomes soar in the past 30 years work in the financial sector. The share of the economy accounted for by salaries and profits in this sector has multiplied. Yet the core function of the finance sector—providing the liquidity and risk-management that eases investment in capital and equipment for other sectors—has not been performed any more efficiently over these three decades.

After the Great Depression saw an unregulated financial sector collapse and contribute to bringing down the rest of the economy, regulations were put into place to prevent a repeat performance. These regulations worked well—large-scale financial crises in the U.S. economy were rare and did not threaten to bring down the larger economy for decades after the Great Depression. Starting in the late 1970s, however, these rules have been under constant assault. By the early 2000s, the Federal Reserve Chairman Alan Greenspan has stated that he assumed this sector's own "self-interest" to be sufficient to ensure stability in the sector, and even in 2008 he wrote that he feared a "casualty" of the financial crisis would be "financial self-regulation, as the fundamental balance mechanism for global finance." The wholesale dismantling of these rules led to huge increases in the sector's returns, but hindsight shows that these gains were due predominantly to taking on riskier bets, which paid off big in the short-run but then blew up. Clearly, the dismantling of these rules did not serve the broader economy well.

The intersection of globalization and a deregulated financial sector meant that even international lending went almost completely unsupervised. When many of the important trading partners of the United States (most notably China) began buying trillions of dollars of dollar-denominated assets, this presented policy makers a clear choice. They chose the short-term preferences of the financial sector over the short-term preferences of the manufacturing sector *and* the long-run health of the overall economy.

This purchase of dollar-denominated debt helped U.S. financial firms by providing them access to cheap money that they could then lend out at a premium. But these purchases also hammered manufacturing firms and their workers producing in the United States, as they led to a large increase in the value of the U.S. dollar. The rising dollar made U.S. exports expensive on world markets while other nations' imports became artificially cheap to American consumers. The result was a trade deficit and hemorrhaging jobs in American manufacturing. Besides presenting this trade-off, the foreign borrowing was also providing further fuel for the housing bubble and was clearly not sustainable in the longer run. So did the economic policy-making elite call for an end to this destructive pattern of international lending? They did not—instead they made up rationales for why there was no housing bubble, why the trade deficits caused by foreign lending were just fine, and why U.S. manufacturing was doomed no matter what.

Abandoning full employment as a target

This pattern of choosing the policy preferences of those in finance over those of workers can also be seen in the push over the past three decades to redefine the central mandate of the Federal Reserve. The Fed's role has been narrowed to targeting a very low rate of inflation rather than pursuing policies that would promote full employment for the American workforce. Despite the fact that the Humphrey-Hawkins Act of 1978 (since expired) called for "full employment" to be a goal for economic policy makers, after the 1970s, a decade that saw inflation erode the returns to lenders, the Federal

Reserve has repeatedly chosen to sacrifice full employment in the name of fighting (real or imagined) inflation.

Since the bargaining power of low- and middle-income workers is most affected by the unemployment rate, a government policy that de-emphasizes the importance of a low unemployment rate harms them the most. In recent decades, many economists and the policy-making elite ratified this shift by claiming that the "natural rate of employment"—the rate of unemployment below which inflation would begin to accelerate— had risen over time, and that any attempt to push unemployment back down to levels frequently enjoyed in the 1950s and 1960s would unleash galloping inflation. Critics of this view were labeled modern-day Luddites, yet a brief episode in the middle and late 1990s proved the supposed Luddites correct.

Buoyed by a bubble in the stock market that began inflating historically quickly in the mid-1990s, demand in the U.S. economy actually began growing fast enough for the unemployment rate to fall well below what economists had claimed would spark inflation. Federal Reserve Chair Alan Greenspan decided not to short-circuit this growth. While this growth was based on an unsustainable foundation and eventually faltered, during the time the economy grew quickly, the unemployment rate dipped below 4% for a time and wage growth was rapid across the board. The end of this boom was *not* caused by an economy overheating due to inflationary pressures spurred by the low unemployment rate—on the contrary, inflation did not budge even as the unemployment rate fell. Instead, the bursting of the stock market bubble brought the boom to an end.

The lessons of this episode should be clear: (a) fast growth and low unemployment are necessary for broad-based wage growth and *can be accommodated without sparking inflation*, but (b) we need to find more sustainable ways to support this growth than bubbles in financial markets.

FIGURE 20

Declining minimum wage
The real value of the minimum wage, 1960-2009

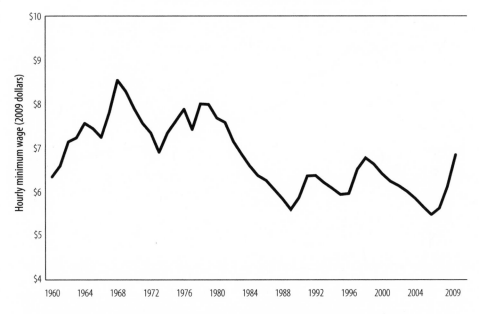

Source: U.S. Department of Labor, Wage, and Hour Division and Bureau of Labor Statistics.

Figure 20: After each legislated increase, inflation naturally erodes the purchasing power of the minimum wage. Long periods of neglect in the 1980s, 1990s, and 2000s led to it reaching its lowest level on record in 2006. And even increases since then have kept it far below its historic peak.

FIGURE 21

Declining unionization
Union coverage rate in the United States, 1973-2009

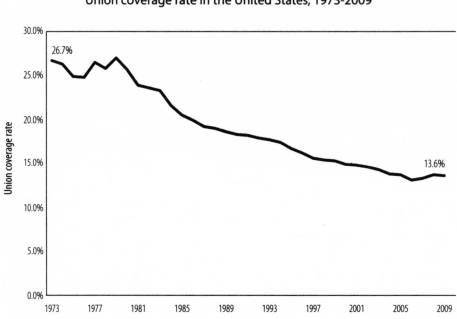

Note: Data for years 1973-76 were imputed using the annual percent change in union membership for those years.
Source: Hirsch and Macpherson (2010) and Bureau of Labor Statistics

Figure 21: Union coverage has steadily eroded since 1973.

FIGURE 22

Growing integration into the global economy
Imports and exports as a percent of GDP, 1947-present

Source: Bureau of Economic Analysis data.

Figure 22: A growing share of the U.S. economy has been integrated into a global economy that is much poorer on average.

FIGURE 23

Less manufacturing, more finance
Manufacturing and financial sectors as share of private economy*

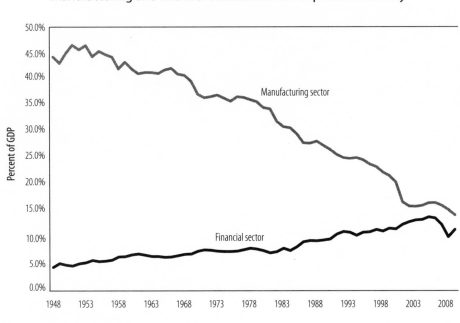

*Compensation plus corporate profits only.

Source: EPI analysis of Bureau of Economic Analysis data.

Figure 23: Starting in the 1980s, the share of the economy accounted for by the financial sector began rising, while the steady-but-measured decline of manufacturing's share sped up radically. By the 2000s, the two sectors were of roughly equal heft.

FIGURE 24

Missing the target
The NAIRU versus actual unemployment rate

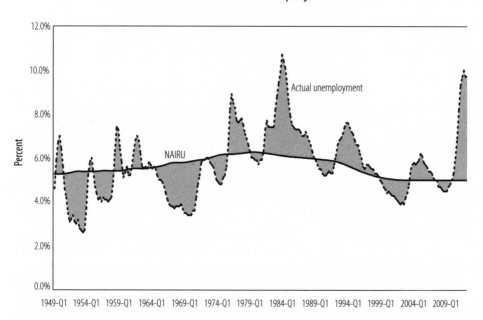

Source: Congressional Budget Office and Bureau of Labor Statistics data.

Figure 24: The official estimate of the "NAIRU"—the rate of unemployment below which the economy cannot go without sparking galloping inflation—is often too high and keeps policy makers from providing jobs to all who want one. However, the past 30 years has seen even this conservative target being routinely missed on the high side. The previous 30 years saw actual rates below the NAIRU as often as above. Not so since.

You get the economy you *choose*

All of these policy choices—what is the value of the minimum wage; the legal boundaries regarding the fight between workers and employers over union organizing; which American workers are provided bulwarks against the pressures of globalization; how much freedom the financial sector has to self-regulate; how much oversight there is over international trade and lending patterns; what is the appropriate inflation level and what is the appropriate unemployment rate—are *choices*, not weather patterns.

These choices—while designed to do something else—were sold to the public based on promises that they would unleash a flood of economic efficiency and boost living standards for everyone. They have manifestly failed to deliver for most working Americans. Growth in productivity—how much income can be generated in an hour of work—slowed even while the fruits of this slower increase were claimed by a smaller, privileged slice of the American economy.

This failure, however, does not guarantee that these choices will be reversed, for while their result has been disastrous for the typical American family, it has been an unalloyed boon for the economic elite. Changing course will require the richest among us to get used to income growth that more closely matches that seen by their fellow Americans. It will require that the barriers they have erected to keep their own incomes safe from real competition are dismantled. Lastly, it will require that they accept the need to prevent or limit many of the financial activities that led to stratospheric incomes, in order to keep them from harming the broader economy.

Reversing the economic strategy of the past three decades, one supported by the richest and most powerful, won't be easy. What the Great Recession has shown, however, is that it is *necessary*. Besides failing to deliver broad-based growth in living standards, this strategy relied on ever-rising debt and asset market bubbles that were allowed to inflate to disastrous proportions to keep consumers buying and the economy humming. These are not durable foundations for growth.

Going forward, growth should be based on widespread wage gains for all workers who will use them to purchase a rising living standard without taking on more and more debt. This task will be easier if rising wages are accompanied by guarantees of basic economic security—that sickness, injury, or other instances of plain bad luck will not consign one to poverty for a lifetime.

An economy based on broad prosperity and security, rather than one based on small pockets of opulence surrounded by insecurity and struggle, will not just make us a better society, it will make our economy more stable and prevent another Great Recession. If there is anything we should have learned from the past two years, it is the importance of not trying to build the economy's foundation in sand.

Incomes in the 30 years before the Great Recession: growing slower and less equal

In the quarter-century between 1947 and 1973, economic growth was both rapid and distributed equally across income classes. The poorest 20% of families saw growth at least as rapid as the richest 20% of families, and everybody in between experienced similar rates of living standards' growth.

Since then, growth in average living standards has unambiguously slowed. Between 1973 and 1995, growth in productivity, or how much income can be generated in each hour of work, collapsed to less than half the rate that characterized the previous quarter-century. Since 1995, productivity growth has risen sharply but remains well below the progress that prevailed between 1947 and 1973.

And this slower growth has been accompanied by a stunning rise in inequality. The growth of typical families' incomes, which once mirrored overall productivity growth, began flattening in the late 1970s, falling far behind productivity growth. And the poorest families saw income growth that lagged families in the middle of the income scale, who in turn lagged the richest families.

The upward march of inequality has not been totally uninterrupted: when between 1996 and 2000 the Federal Reserve allowed unemployment rates to creep down well below what most economists insisted was possible, wages across the board began rising at a brisk pace. This was just one stark reminder that economic policy matters for both the pace and distribution of economic growth.

However, after a brief decline in inequality following the stock market crash of 2001, the older patterns reasserted themselves and inequality began marching upward faster than ever. It is this inequality and slowdown in productivity that is the clearest evidence that, from the perspective of typical American families, our economy has been underperforming relative to its potential for decades *before* the Great Recession.

FIGURE 25

"Fast-and-fair" versus "slow-and-skewed"
Real family income growth by quintile, 1947-73 and 1979-2009

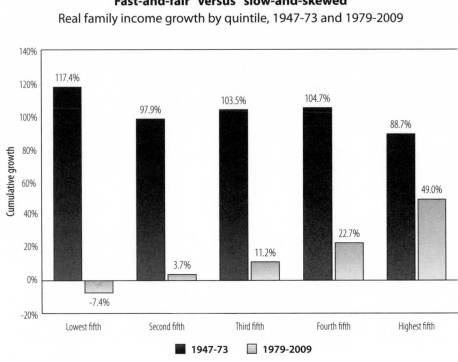

Source: : EPI analysis of U.S. Census Bureau data.

Figure 25: Fast-and-fair income growth versus slow-and-skewed. The "picket fence" bars—those columns showing income growth from 1947-73, are both higher in each quintile and of roughly even heights. The "staircase" bars—those columns showing income growth from 1979-2009, are lower for each quintile but showing faster growth the farther up the income scale you go.

FIGURE 26

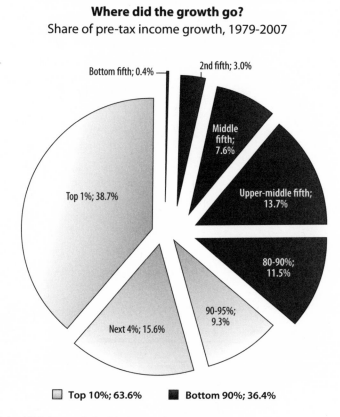

Where did the growth go?
Share of pre-tax income growth, 1979-2007

Bottom fifth; 0.4%

2nd fifth; 3.0%

Middle fifth; 7.6%

Upper-middle fifth; 13.7%

Top 1%; 38.7%

80-90%; 11.5%

90-95%; 9.3%

Next 4%; 15.6%

☐ Top 10%; 63.6%   ■ Bottom 90%; 36.4%

Source: EPI analysis of CBO Average Federal Tax Rates and Income, 2010.

Figure 26: The top 10% of the income distribution has claimed just under *two-thirds* of all income gains since 1979, with the top 1% alone claiming just under 40% of overall gains.

FIGURE 27

Small groups get the biggest gains
Change in average, pre-tax household income
by income group, 1979-2005

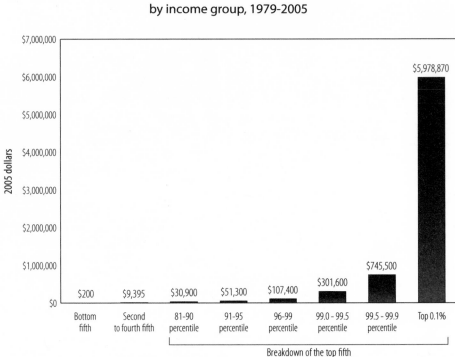

Source: EPI analysis of Congressional Budget Office data.

Figure 27: The dollar increases associated with rising inequality are staggering. This graph shows the rise in average incomes between 1979 and 2005 at different points of the income distribution. The bottom 20% saw $200 gains over the entire quarter-century. The top 1% saw average gains over $1 million, with the top 0.1% seeing gains of over $5 million, the next richest 0.4% seeing gains of over $700,000 and the next richest 0.5% seeing gains of over $300,000.

FIGURE 28

What has rise of finance bought? Not greater fixed investment
Fixed investment and finance sector value-added as shares of GDP

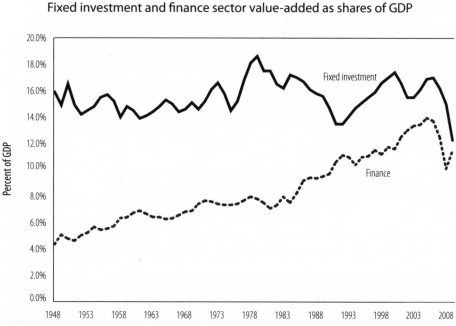

Source: EPI analysis of Bureau of Economic Analysis data.

Figure 28: Given that finance is an intermediate input, meant to just grease the wheels of firms' ability to make capital purchases, it's worth seeing if the rise of finance led to a marked increase in investment in plants and equipment. This graph shows that as the share of finance in the economy rose, the share of business fixed investment did not. We should ask why we are directing so much money toward the financial sector.

Is everybody getting richer but the rich are just getting richer faster?

Some would argue that obsessing over the incomes of the very top just represents envy, and that what should matter is simply the pace of improvement for typical families. In short, if everybody is getting richer but the rich are just getting richer faster, what's the problem? The problem with this view, crudely put, is that since 1979 the rich have grabbed so much of overall income growth that there is just not enough left over to allow most American families' incomes to grow faster than a crawl. The arithmetic of this is pretty easy to understand: when overall income growth is just under 3% per year, and the richest 10%, who already control a third of all income, start claiming gains of 5% per year, the rest of the population will only see growth of just over 1% per year, less than half the overall rate. This is essentially what happened between 1979 and 2007, with the faster income growth of the richest 10% leading to them claiming almost *two-thirds* of the total income gains during that time.

The economics of how this plays out is perhaps a little harder to grasp than the simple arithmetic, but the important thing to remember is that one person's *wage* is another person's *cost*. Therefore, slow growth in the wages of autoworkers is bad for *them* but *good* for those buying a car, while fast growth of wages of finance professionals is good for them but bad for firms and households seeking financial services.

A key reason why, for example, lawyers and surgeons saw rapidly rising living standards over the past three decades is *precisely because* the wages and salaries of the majority of American workers did not rise as rapidly as theirs. Because the wages of autoworkers and landscapers grew slowly, cars and lawn-care services became relatively cheap, boosting the living standards of workers not concentrated in those professions. Lawyers, surgeons, and financial professionals could enjoy goods and services that were made cheap because the workers producing them saw such slow wage growth, all while seeing their own salaries move briskly ahead.

In short, having the already-privileged grab a growing share of the economic pie over time simply leaves less of it for everybody else, and given the overall rate of income growth over the past 30 years, the only way that low- and middle-income families could have seen *more* income growth is if very high-income families saw *less*. Wanting to see slower income-growth at the very top is not driven by envy, instead it is just driven by a simple recognition that more at the top means less at the middle and bottom.

FIGURE 29

The $9,220 inequality tax
Real median family income and income assuming growth rate of average income

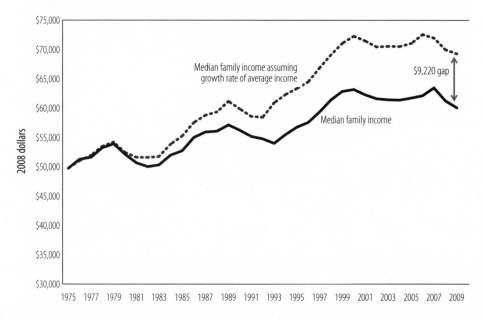

Source: EPI analysis of U.S. Census Bureau data.

Figure 29: This figure shows how increases at the top squeeze growth in the middle. The lines show actual growth in median family incomes as well as the growth that would have prevailed had there been no increase in inequality over the period—that is, if all incomes had just grown at the overall average rate. Had this happened, the median family today would have incomes 14% higher—equal to $9,220.

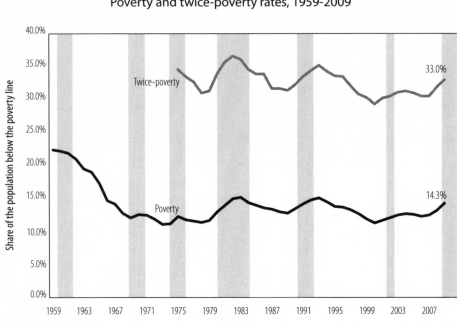

FIGURE 30

When jobs go down, poverty goes up
Poverty and twice-poverty rates, 1959-2009

Note: Shaded areas denote recession.

Source: U.S. Census Bureau, Historical Poverty Tables.

Figure 30: Incomes at the bottom have been squeezed even harder. Even as GDP per worker has grown by nearly 60% since 1975, the share of people living in poverty or with incomes less than twice the poverty rate has actually risen.

FIGURE 31

Another inequality tax—poverty no longer falls as economy grows
Actual and simulated poverty, 1959-2009

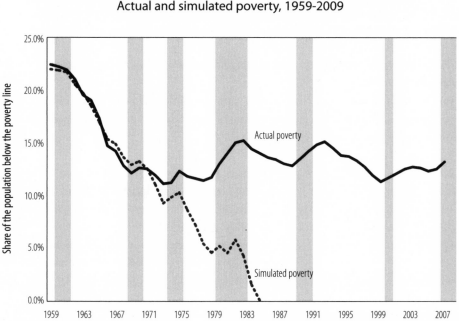

Note: Shaded areas denote recession.

Source: Actual poverty from U.S. Census Bureau. Simulated poverty based on regression of actual poverty with per capita GDP through 1973, from the Bureau of Economic Analysis, and then used to predict poverty rates in subsequent years from that model. For more on this method, see Danziger and Gottschalk (1996).

Figure 31: Growing inequality has contributed to the severing of the link between overall growth and progress in reducing poverty. If the relationship between overall GDP growth and poverty that prevailed between 1959 and 1973 had held up, the poverty rate would have been driven to zero by the late 1980s. Sadly, it *didn't* hold up, and instead progress in reducing poverty was halted in its tracks.

Why have typical families' incomes and overall economic growth de-linked?

There are two ways to answer why typical families' incomes and overall economic growth no longer march in lock-step: one is facile and based on simple arithmetic, and the other is much more complex and important.

The arithmetic of rising inequality: falling wage growth for most American workers

The simplest answer as to why median family income no longer keeps up with pro-ductivity growth is that the growth in hourly wages of workers has collapsed relative to the quarter-century after World War II.

Again, the full-employment period between 1996 and 2000 is a shining exception to this, but largely the past 30 years have been a wage disaster for many American workers. And if *wages* are not rising, then *incomes* can generally only rise if individu-als work longer hours. The fact that today's working families stress about a "time-squeeze" is no surprise—the wage collapse has meant that longer working hours have become the only way most working families could get robust income gains in recent decades.

The economics of rising inequality

So it is clear that wage and compensation growth for American workers has collapsed and that this has put a heavy drag on overall income growth. Why did this happen?

A predictable response to the observation that most workers' wages no longer keep pace with productivity growth is to blame the victim. The simplest blame-game is to assert that American workers have a skills problem: that well-paying jobs are avail-able, but that American workers just don't qualify for them anymore.

It is hard to accept this story in the face of a steady increase in the share of American workers with a college degree. It is even harder to accept it when one sees that even the wages of the typical college graduate have performed poorly relative to productiv-ity growth.

A more convincing story would focus on the full range of economic policies and de-velopments that affect the bargaining position of rank-and-file American workers vis-à-vis their employers and the economy's elite. All of the policy choices of the past 30

FIGURE 32

The wedge between overall and individual prosperity
Growth of production worker compensation and productivity, 1947-2009

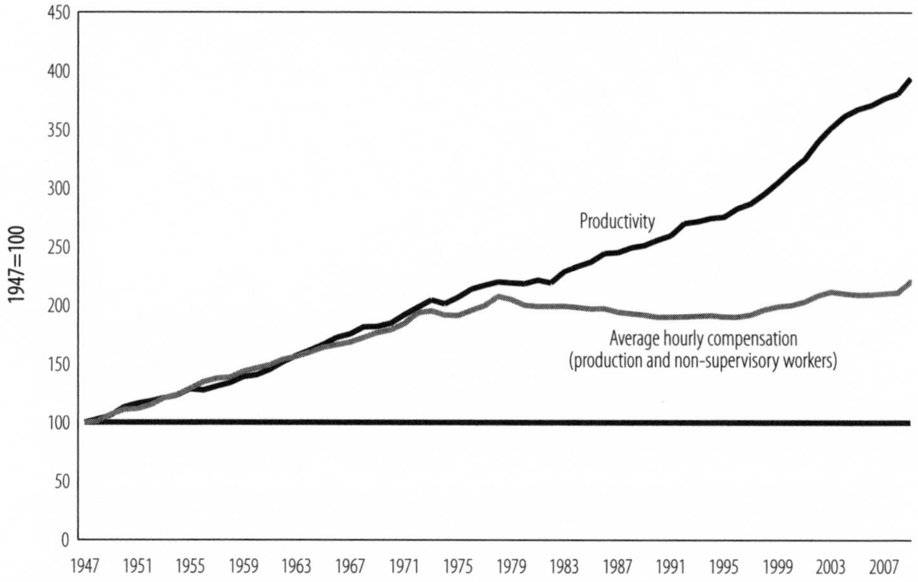

Source: EPI analysis of Bureau of Labor Statistics and Bureau of Economic Analysis data.

Figure 32: The broken link between hourly compensation growth for rank-and-file workers and overall productivity growth explains much of the rise in family income inequality. Production and non-supervisory workers constitute 80% of private-sector workers and growth in their compensation, which once tracked overall productivity closely, has all but flatlined in the past quarter-century.

FIGURE 33

Not just about getting a college degree
Median hourly compensation by educational attainment
and productivity growth, 1973-2009

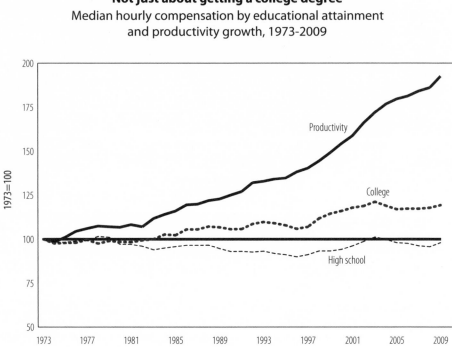

Source: EPI analysis of Bureau of Labor Statistics and Bureau of Economic Analysis data.

Figure 33: The rise of inequality is often attributed to the failure of American workers' skills. Besides just being false in its premise (the share of the workforce with a college degree has nearly doubled since 1973) it also fails to recognize that even median college wages have seen poor performance in recent decades and have lagged productivity growth by a(n) (un)healthy margin.

FIGURE 34

Even the 95th percentile does not see wages keep up with productivity

Hourly wage and productivity growth by wage percentile, 1973-2009

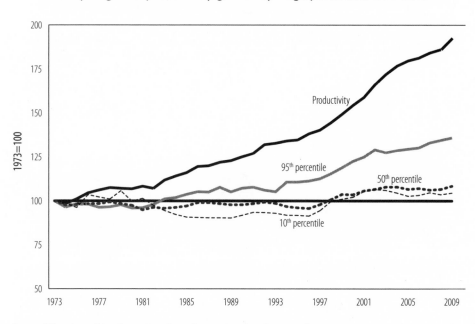

Source: EPI analysis of the Current Population Survey, Outgoing Rotations Group.

Figure 34: How high up the wage scale do you have to go before seeing wages that track productivity growth? Past the 95th percentile.

FIGURE 35

Low-wage workers more vulnerable to unemployment changes
Percentage change in male and female wages given 1 percentage-point
decline in unemployment rate, by wage decile

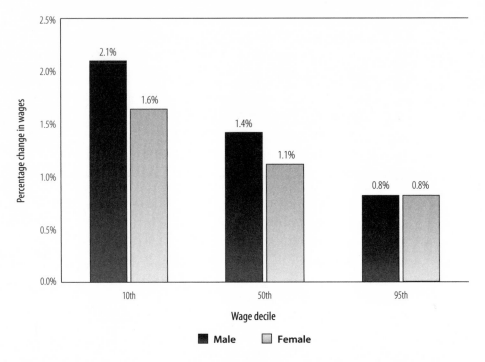

Source: EPI analysis of Bureau of Labor Statistics and Current Population Survey, Outgoing Rotation Group data.

Figure 35: Failure to target low unemployment hurts lower-wage workers the most. This graph shows the responsiveness of wages to changes in unemployment at different points on the wage scale. Low-wage workers' wages are most sensitive to the overall unemployment rate.

FIGURE 36

Falling unionization rates hurt lowest earners the most
Union wage premium by wage percentile

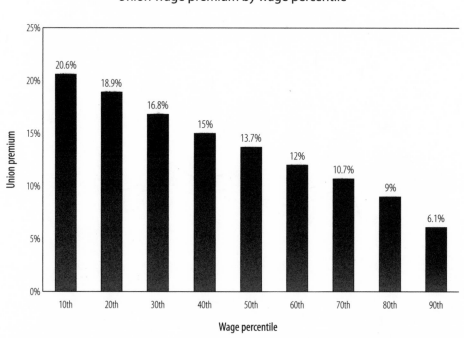

Source: Schmitt (2008).

Figure 36: De-unionization hurts low-wage earners the most. This figure shows the union wage premium—that is the higher wages associated with being in a union even after controlling for individual characteristics like education and age—at different points in the wage distribution. Union membership is associated with the largest boost to wages at the lower percentiles of the distribution.

FIGURE 37

The globalization tax for rank-and-file workers
Annual earnings for full-time, median wage earner

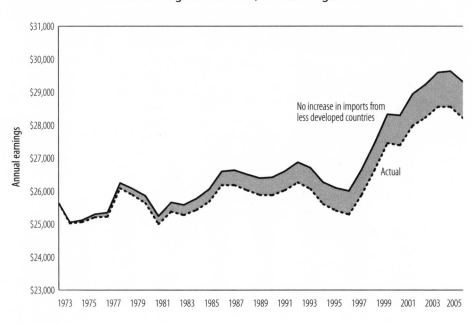

Source: Bivens (2008).

Figure 37: While growing global integration explains only a minority share of the total rise in inequality, this still adds up to real money for most American workers. This graph draws on the work of Bivens (2008) to show the annual earnings of a median wage-earner working full-time—both actual earnings since 1973 and those that would have prevailed had there been no increase in imports from poorer countries pressuring their wages.

FIGURE 38

More compensation heading to the very top
Ratio of average CEO total direct compensation to average
production worker compensation, 1965-2009

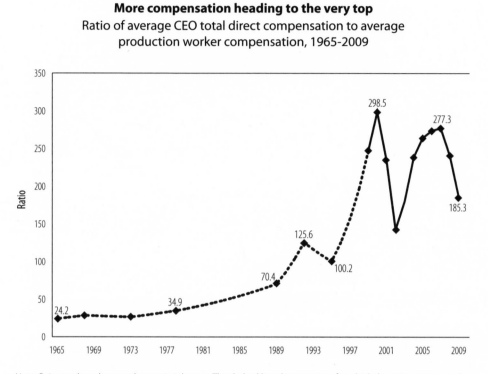

Note: Point markers denote where ratio is known. The dashed line denotes years for which the ratio was imputed.
Source: Authors' analysis of *Wall Street Journal*/Mercer, Hay Group (2010).

Figure 38: CEOs have always made much more money than the workers they supervise. But the last three decades have seen this ratio explode.

FIGURE 39

The premium to working in finance
Ratio of earnings per full-time worker in finance versus
the rest of the private sector

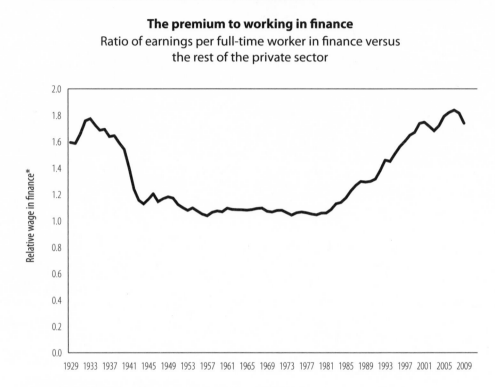

* Ratio of compensation per full-time employee in finance relative to other private industries.
Source: EPI analysis of Bureau of Economic Analysis data.

Figure 39: As finance grew as a share of the economy and was de-regulated beginning in the late 1970s, compensation per employee in finance, which had roughly been at parity with the rest of the private sector for decades, soared past levels even seen in the run-up to the Great Depression.

years have actually not only failed to spur faster growth, but each one has also put downward pressure on the wage growth of typical American workers. One begins to sense that this was by design.

The full-employment wage boom of the late 1990s was noted earlier. A growing body of evidence shows that persistently high unemployment hurts wage growth, and this impact is not equally felt across all workers in the labor force. Lower-wage workers are hurt more by high unemployment, while high-wage workers are hurt less. The shift in economic policy that made low inflation instead of low unemployment the chief concern of macroeconomic policy has hence constituted a powerful blow to American workers' wages, especially for the most vulnerable workers.

The decline in reach of key labor market institutions—especially unions and the minimum wage—have also exerted a powerful drag on American wages. As union membership declined and the value of the minimum wage was allowed to erode through inflation over the past 30 years, the bargaining position of tens of millions workers has predictably suffered.

Globalization, especially globalization governed by rules that protect the interests of the corporate class while making no attempt to shield vulnerable American workers, has also constituted a powerful drag on American wages in recent decades.

Lower wage growth did not buy greater economic security or sustained progress in closing racial gaps

If lower wage growth had somehow purchased other elements of economic security over the past 30 years, then the story might be a bit brighter. Unfortunately, slower wage growth has instead gone hand-in-hand with heightened economic insecurity for many American families.

While the long-run trend has seen wages grow more slowly on average, the yearly volatility of these changes has unambiguously increased. The trend in Americans covered by health insurance has largely stagnated in recent decades (and has been made much worse by the Great Recession), and it is only the expansion of public insurance programs like Medicare and Medicaid that have kept coverage rates from outright deteriorating. A shrinking share of American workers are covered by a retirement plan of any kind, and those who do have a retirement plan generally have riskier defined-contribution plans rather than more-reliable defined-benefit plans. Even growth in

FIGURE 40

Three decades with no improvement in health coverage
Share of under-65 population without health insurance coverage, 1959-2007

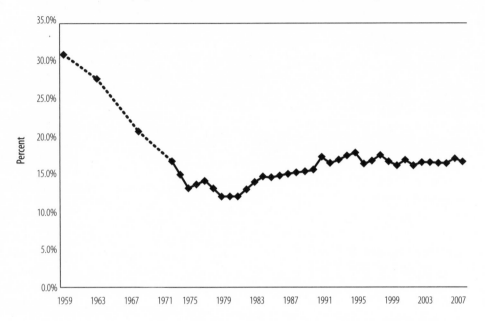

Note: First three data points (1959, 1963, and 1968) refer only to coverage for hospital insurance. Dotted lines indicate no available data.

Source: National Health Insurance Survey and Cohen et al. (2009).

Figure 40: Health insurance coverage for the under-65 population has shown no substantive improvement over the past two decades. The over-65 population, it should be remembered, has universal coverage financed through a single-payer public system (Medicare).

FIGURE 41

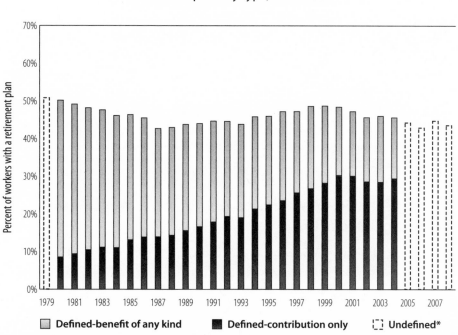

Pension coverage—roughly flat but riskier
Retirement plans by type, 1979-2008

Defined-benefit of any kind   Defined-contribution only   Undefined*

* Unable to distinguish between DB and DC plans in these years

Source: EPI analysis of March CPS data and Center for Retirement Research data.

Figure 41: Fewer workers have employer-provided pension plans of any type and of those workers who are enrolled, defined-contribution plans that shift more risk onto workers have become more prevalent.

life expectancy in the past quarter-century has been heavily skewed toward the more-privileged end of the income distribution.

Furthermore, slower wage-growth was not accompanied by much meaningful progress on closing racial gaps in unemployment, family income, or net worth. In a country where different races often experience very different economic outcomes, a sad commonality is that the past three decades have been a disappointing period of economic stagnation. A particularly striking fact concerns the unemployment experience of African Americans, a group who has seen an average unemployment rate roughly double the white rate for decades. The full complement (53 weeks worth) of "emergency" unemployment compensation was automatically triggered in the Great Recession in states where the overall unemployment rate exceeded 8.5%. However, the unemployment rate for African Americans has been lower than 8.5% for only 45 of the 369 months since 1979, or roughly 12% of the time.

How did American families cope with lower wage-growth and rising insecurity?

As wage-growth slowed, American families coped in a number of ways. They worked more. They saved less. They took on debt.

Working more helped for years: by adding hundreds of hours of paid work time to their lives, many families were able to boost income. Of course, there's a limit to working more hours as a coping strategy—once every adult member of a household becomes a full-time worker, it becomes impossible to boost income growth by continually piling on more hours. In short, unless American families learn to live without sleep or we repeal child labor laws, there is little room to boost incomes by working more.

The decline in savings and the rise in debt also have limits, as demonstrated clearly in the Great Recession. Rising private debt (both household and business) depends on a financial sector willing to extend loans. If the willingness to extend these loans is built on myopic expectations about the future (say, on the expectation that home prices will rise forever) then rapid reversals, leading to wrenching adjustments for the economy, are bound to happen. And they did…and the Great Recession began.

But, for years bubbles in the financial sector—the stock market bubble of the late 1990s as well as the housing market bubble of the 2000s—kept the finance sector willing to extend loans and kept the economy from running aground. Financialization—

FIGURE 42

Even life expectancy gains are unequal
Life expectancy for male Social Security–covered workers (age 60)
by earnings group, 1972 and 2001

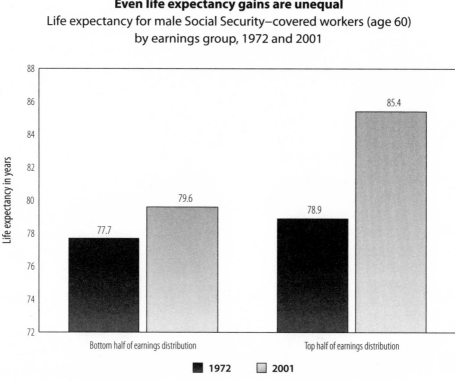

Source: EPI analysis of Waldron (2007).

Figure 42: Even gains in life expectancy have been inequitably distributed in recent decades. The bottom half of the earnings distribution has seen gains of less than two years while those in the top half have seen gains of 6.5 years.

FIGURE 43

Before the Great Recession, Americans saved less to consume more
Personal savings rate*

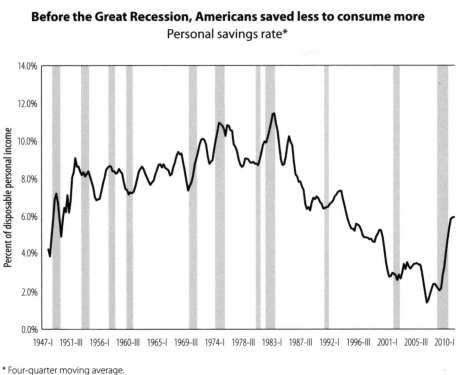

* Four-quarter moving average.

Note: Shaded areas denote recessions.

Source: Bureau of Economic Analysis data.

Figure 43: Before the Great Recession, the personal savings rate was on a steady decline since the early 1980s. Since the Great Recession began, households have cut back on spending and begun serious saving again. While good for the long-term, this shock to consumer spending is a large part of what caused the Great Recession.

FIGURE 44

Debt rises as income growth slows

The ratio of household liabilities to disposable personal income, 1945-2009

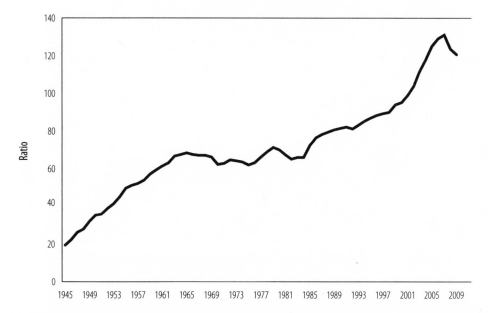

Source: EPI analysis of Bureau of Economic Analysis and Federal Reserve Flow of Funds data.

Figure 44: Less savings and slower income growth have translated into a steep rise in the ratio of debt to personal income over the quarter-century before the Great Recession. That this has reversed even in the face of falling personal income is a testament to how quickly households have begun shedding debt in the past 2 years.

FIGURE 45

In the late 1990s, the stock bubble substitutes for savings
Cyclically adjusted price earnings ratio, 1947-2009

Source: Robert Shiller (2010).

Figure 45: Households could save less and still be on track to meet wealth goals (retirement, putting kids through college) for a time because the stock market bubble greatly increased net worth. This bubble burst in 2001 and the stock market took another downward jump in 2008.

FIGURE 46

In the 2000s, the housing market bubble substitutes for savings

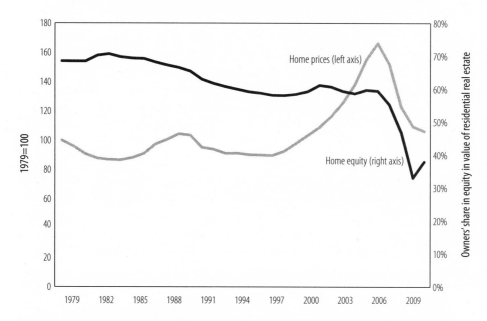

Note: Home equity is a measure of the share of owners' equity relative to the total value of residential real estate. Price index is a measure of the inflation-adjusted price of homes.

Source: Home equity as share of value of real estate from the Federal Reserve, home price index from Shiller (http://www.econ.yale.edu/~shiller/data.htm).

Figure 46: Even as homes began being worth more and more in the 2000s, the share of owners' equity in real estate actually fell. This is testament to how much of that equity was being stripped out of homes and feeding economic growth through the decade. The burst of the home-price bubble has led to a precipitous drop in owners' equity.

that is, the growing importance of the finance sector in the overall economy—hence became an important part of the coping mechanisms that allowed the economy to grow for a time even as most households in it were not seeing incomes grow as fast as the surrounding economy.

In the end, however, financialization was not a durable pillar for growth. Besides providing little in the way of benefits beyond enriching a very select few, making the economy dependent on ever-rising asset prices carried the seeds of its own destruction. Eventually, the economy must run on demand—growth that is sustainable and purchased out of current wages and incomes and not out of paper gains extracted from rising home prices.

Of course, we need to be careful not to throw out the baby with the bathwater: the tech-led stock market bubble, for example, actually supported the full-employment wage-boom of the late 1990s. While the source of this boom was clearly unsustainable in hindsight, there is no reason to think there is anything about low unemployment and robust wage growth *per se* that is unsustainable; rather they need to be attained by an economy that generates wages and incomes to support the typical family's growth in living standards, not paper gains extracted from bubbles in home or stock prices.

Where to from Here?

The pressures placed on America's working families by economic policies that produced slow-and-unequal growth ended up not just stressing them, but also breaking the economy. And there is little relief on the horizon.

In August 2010, the unemployment rate stood at 9.6%, essentially the same level it had been a year before. Most forecasts (private and public) for 2011 project that it will be at essentially the same level a year from now. The economic challenges over the next few years are daunting; just returning to the 2007 *status quo* will take several more years. But even this won't be enough—we need to build a new economy that works better for America's working families. Choices need to be made that benefit all of working America—not just the rich and powerful. And if this is to be done, we will have to design an economy that just works better and no longer risks a repeat of the Great Recession.

Think of the American economy like a patient suffering from chronic ailments driven largely by bad choices—smoking, eating unhealthy foods, and not exercising. Then he makes another bad decision and decides to take up swimming with sharks, whereupon he is promptly bitten. The clear priority is to staunch the bleeding coming from the shark-bite—until this wound is healed, there can be no serious progress made in addressing the chronic ailments. But once it *is* healed, this patient also needs help quickly to reverse the bad decisions that led to his chronic ailments.

Today's policy-making elite are severely underestimating both the wound and the chronic ailments. While much has been done to combat the recession, the urgency policy makers feel has clearly waned and the economy is assumed to be on a path to recovery. This is a very premature diagnosis: mainstream, private-sector forecasts predict that unemployment will be higher in 2011 than it was in 2010, and that 2011 will see the highest full-year unemployment rate since the Bureau of Labor Statistics began consistent tracking in 1948, higher than the worst year of the early 1980s recession. And in 2012, the unemployment rate will be higher than the worst year of the early 1990s recession. And even in 2013, the unemployment rate will be higher than the worst year of the early 2000s recession, *six full years after the Great Recession began*. In short, it is far too early to declare the patient stable.

Clear economic remedies exist. The economy needs more demand for goods and services, and the full support of fiscal, monetary, and exchange rate policies have yet to be deployed to generate this demand. But, politics and ideology lie in the way. And as is usually the case, in a contest between good economics and bad politics, politics seems to win every time. But there should be no mistake: tolerating an agonizingly slow recovery from the Great Recession is a choice, not an inevitability.

Perhaps one last illustration of the perverse choices made in the U.S. economy in recent decades will make the point. The worst year of the early 2000s recession and recovery for the unemployment rate came in 2003, when the unemployment rate reached 6.0%. This level of unemployment was cited to support adding $350 billion to the national debt by cutting taxes (the Jobs and Growth Tax Relief and Reconciliation Act of 2003, or JGTRRA). These tax cuts overwhelmingly benefited richer taxpayers and provided very little actual job creation, yet Congress enacted them. But despite the fact that the unemployment rate is now forecast to be just under 10% in 2011, Congress seems unwilling to take action that is anywhere near as large as JGTRRA, even though today's crisis is clearly more acute and there are many effective job creators that could be financed with JGTRRA-sized fiscal support for the economy. Again, the economy's current distressed state is a result of choices, not inevitability.

The rush to declare the fallout from the Great Recession over would be more forgivable (though no less unwise) if it were done in the name of trying to reverse the bad decisions that had led to the chronic ailments of slow growth and rising inequality. But, just as policy makers are constrained by political and ideological orthodoxy in fighting the immediate effects of the Great Recession, most seem just as limited in what they view as necessary for the economy going forward.

Building an economy that reliably generates rising living standards for all will require choosing a very different path. The value of the minimum wage should be raised and then indexed to keep up with wider economic growth instead of being subject to the whim of politicians who aren't concerned about the plight of our lowest-wage workers. The laws governing workplaces should be changed so that workers who want to join a union can exercise that choice without taking heroic risks in the face of employer resistance. Americans should be guaranteed that their retirement and health security will not be fatally compromised by a run of bad luck or an unscrupulous employer or insurance company. Economic elites should not be allowed to decide which parts of the American economy should be integrated into a much poorer global economy and which parts should be shielded from this integration without taking into account the effects of such decisions for all of America's workers. The excesses of the financial sector should be reined in. International capital flows should be monitored and managed to keep them from wreaking havoc both here and abroad. Ambitious investments—many public—should be made in the country's infrastructure, especially for education and meeting the needs of a greener economy. Full employment should again be enshrined as a policy target for which the Federal Reserve and other policy makers are accountable. Lastly, closing the troubling racial gaps in employment, wages, and net worth should be a primary target for policy makers.

All of these changes will serve to tip the balance of economic power away from the privileged few who have done so well for the past 30 years and back toward everybody else. This won't be easy—while the privileged are few, their resources are vast and they have been able to convince the policy-making class in Washington, D.C. that their preferences are the only road to economic success. In a sense they are right: their preferences are the only road that leads to such extravagant economic success for them. But this road also leads to a dead-end for too many working Americans. It's time we chose another one.

All of this will require affirmative choices to take the economy in a different direction—it will not happen on its own. But just as the policies designed to enrich the few while leaving the rest behind over the past 30 years succeeded in that aim, different choices that are designed to reverse this pattern of gains can also work. Even better, they can work not just to provide faster growth in the living standards of typical American families, but also to provide a more stable economy that is less prone to spectacular crack-ups like the Great Recession.

Bibliography

Bivens, Josh. 2008. *Everybody Wins, Except for Most of Us: What Economics Teaches About Globalization*. Washington, D.C.: Economic Policy Institute.

Blinder, Alan S., and Mark Zandi. 2010. "How the Great Recession Was Brought to an End." Working Paper.

Cohen, Robin A., Diane M. Makuc, Amy B. Bernstein, Linda T. Bilheimer, and Eve Powell-Griner. 2009. *Health Insurance Coverage Trends, 1959–2007: Estimates from the National Health Interview Survey*. National Health Statistics Reports, No. 17. Hyattsville, MD: Centers for Disease Control and Prevention.

Danziger, Sheldon and Peter Gottschalk. 1996. *America Unequal*. Cambridge: Harvard University Press.

Hirsch, Barry T., and David Machpherson. "Union Membership Coverage, Density, and Employment Among All Wage and Salary Workers, 1973–2010." Union Membership and Coverage Database. http://unionstats.com.

Schmitt, John. 2008. "The Union Wage Advantage for Low-Wage Workers." CEPR Report. Washington D.C.: Center for Economic Policy Research.

Shiller, Robert. 2010. Online updates to data first presented in *Irrational Exuberance*. Princeton University Press. http://www.econ.yale.edu/~shiller/data.htm.

Waldron, Hilary. 2007. Trends in Mortality Differentials and Life Expectancy for Male Social Security-Covered Workers, by Socioeconomic Status. *Social Security Bulletin*, Vol. 678, No. 3.

About EPI

The Economic Policy Institute, a nonprofit Washington D.C. think-tank, was created in 1986 to broaden the discussion about economic policy to include the interests of low- and middle-income workers. Today, with global competition expanding, wage inequality rising, and the methods and nature of work changing in fundamental ways, it is as crucial as ever that people who work for a living have a voice in the economic discourse.

EPI was the first—and remains the premier—think-tank to focus on the economic condition of low- and middle-income Americans and their families. Its careful research on the status of American workers has become the gold standard in that field. EPI researchers, who often testify to Congress and are widely cited in the media, first brought to light the disconnect between pay and productivity that marked the U.S. economy in the 1990s and is now widely recognized as a cause of growing inequality.

EPI's staff includes eight Ph.D.-level researchers, a half dozen policy analysts and research assistants, and a full communications and outreach staff. EPI also works closely with a national network of prominent scholars. The institute conducts original research according to strict standards of objectivity, and couples its findings with outreach and popular education. Its work spans a wide range of economic issues, such as trends in wages, incomes, and prices; health care; education; retirement security; state-level economic development strategies; trade and global finance; comparative international economic performance; the health of manufacturing and other key sectors; global competitiveness; and energy development. Its research is varied, but a common thread runs through it: EPI examines issues through a "living standards" lens by analyzing the impact of policies and initiatives on the American public.

From its findings, EPI publishes books, studies, issue briefs, popular education materials, and other publications; sponsors conferences and seminars; briefs policy makers at all levels of government; provides technical support to national, state, and local activists and community organizations; testifies before national, state, and local legislatures; and provides information and background to the print and electronic media. Over the course of a year, EPI is called upon hundreds of times to inform policy debates, citizens' group meetings, and educational forums.

EPI is typically cited in the media more than 20,000 times per year, including more than 15,000 mentions per year in print and online media. EPI is mentioned and/or its staff are seen or heard by over 300 million television or radio viewers or listeners per year.

EPI has always demanded a high standard of quality in its research because of its desire to be a credible participant in public debates and a reliable source of information and analysis for policy makers, the press, community activists, academics, corporate leaders, labor union officials, and the general public. Its methods for ensuring that its research methodologies and outcomes are exemplary include the use of highly qualified researchers and multiple reviews by outside experts, including those who are known for disagreeing with EPI's values. In-house researchers maintain their standing in the academic community by publishing findings in prestigious peer-reviewed academic journals, like the *American Economic Review* and the *New England Journal of Medicine*.

Its founders include Jeff Faux, EPI's first president; economist Barry Bluestone of Northeastern University; Robert Kuttner, columnist for *Business Week* and *Newsweek* and editor of *The American Prospect*; Ray Marshall, former U.S. secretary of labor and professor at the LBJ School of Public Affairs, University of Texas-Austin; Robert Reich, former U.S. secretary of labor and professor at UC Berkeley; and economist Lester Thurow of the MIT Sloan School of Management.

EPI is a 501(c)(3) corporation. From 2005 through 2007, a majority of its funding (about 53%) was in the form of foundation grants, while another 29% came from labor unions. EPI also receives support from individuals, corporations, and other organizations.

About the Author

JOSH BIVENS joined the Economic Policy Institute in 2002. He is the author of *Everybody Wins Except for Most of Us: What Economics Teaches About Globalization* and has published in both academic and popular venues, including *USA Today*, *The Guardian*, *Challenge*, and *Worth*. He is a frequent commentator on economic issues for a variety of media outlets, including the NewsHour on PBS, the Diane Rehm Show, NPR, CNN, CNBC, Reuters, and the BBC and has testified before Congress. He has previously worked at Roosevelt University in Chicago and for the Congressional Research Service.